YHWH's Unique

Time-Piece

EXPLAINED

YHWH's Unique Time-piece: Explained
© 2017 Diane Covher

Compiled by Diane Covher; January 2016
Revised October 2018
www.therepairerofthebreach.org
E-mail: isa5812@wildblue.net

Sacred Word Publishing
www.sacredwordpublishing.net
SacredWordPublishing@yahoo.com
1st Printing: 2017
978-1-387-17646-5

Where a specific religious observance has been abandoned by the people,

no amount of exegetical authoritarianism can revive it...

Rabbi Shlomo Yitzchaki (Rashi)

(11th Century)

EXEGETICAL, a. Explanatory; tending to unfold or illustrate; expository; Serving to explain; tending to illustrate.

TABLE OF CONTENTS

Foreword

　　"Many believers who find apparent contradictions in the Bible (or their theology), can be shaken. Instead of digging deeper into the truth for the underlying principle that will reconcile the two seemingly contradictory points, they will instead choose to believe the one that agrees with their belief system because it fits the tenor of their feelings and thus they will reject the other. Anything new is taken as unnecessary knowledge. A "mature" believer, after all, has the truth and has no need for more. When some new information comes up that they don't know, they feel "I don't need to know that. If it were important to know I'd already know it, because what I already know is sufficient for salvation and the theology I have been taught has always been sound."

A true searcher of the Word, however, will never reject something simply because it contradicts a preconceived idea or cherished opinion. To him, the truth is more important than anything else. He realizes that not knowing the truth does not change the reality of what is true. Therefore he would want to know the truth. Also, understanding that feelings are not a reliable indication of what is truth, he will chose to follow the light wherever it leads, even if it means laying down his most cherished beliefs." (WLC paraphrased)

The following information in this book will cause you to do either of the ways stated. Either you will feel uncomfortable with the contents and proclaim you do not agree with causing division and discomfort. Or you will be compelled to research it deeper and prove whether it is valid or not. *This one thing is important:* skimming only gives you fuel for an argument......reading gives you understanding.

The following pages contain a compilation of the different writings I have done concerning the calendar time piece of YHWH. I hope that in this work you will find answers to the many questions you have had about this most controversial subject. Please keep in mind that being open to thoroughly examine any FACTS on a subject is being a Proverbs 18:15 person: *Pro 18:15 The heart of the understanding one gets knowledge, And the ear of the wise seeks knowledge.*

I myself would not want to be a Proverbs 18:13 person: *Pro 18:13 He who answers a matter before he hears it, It is folly and shame to him.*

INTRODUCTION

Since 1971, I have walked beside my husband on the path that our Father has set before us and we have not stopped. He has put us together as a team and until we are called home we will walk to His tune. In the year 2011, He revealed a truth to us about His time keeping set at creation and we would like to share it with you.

Rev 18:1 After these things I saw another angel coming down from heaven, having great authority, and the earth was lit up from his splendor. 2 And he cried out with a strong voice, saying, "Babylon the great has fallen, and she has become a dwelling place of demons, a prison for every unclean spirit, and a cage for every unclean and detestable bird! 3 For all the nations have drunk of the wine of the wrath of her fornication, and the kings of the earth have committed fornication with her, and the merchants of the earth have become rich through the wealth of her luxury." 4 And I heard another voice from heaven saying, "Come out of her, my people, lest you participate in her sins, and lest you receive of her plagues.

Come out of her my people. Do we really hear the plea and the seriousness from the Father in this statement? What sins would we be partaking in? What plagues is He talking about?

As many of us opened our eyes and heart to examining the road we were on; we realized through studying different accounts in history the collection of errors of the teachings we walked in. We learned by reading the scriptures through renewed vision of who we truly are as YHWH's seed, that His way, His ancient path has been overgrown with weeds, like the hanging gardens of Babylon, made by man's rules and traditions and cunningly led by the god of this kingdom.

Through hundreds of years of assimilation into the deceptive living of the enemy saying "come lie with me" we have lost YHWH's pure way.

Why is the name Babylon used and applied to this mysterious kingdom we are to flee from? What exactly does "Babylon" mean?

The Strong's concordance tells us it means confusion, to mix, mingle, to overflow as with oil or cover over something or mix like you would fodder which is feed prepared for animals rather than them grazing fresh grass.

Father is pleading with His children to not mix or mingle with the things of this world or to feed on the mixture laid out by the enemy. He wants us to graze on His pure truth.

At the beginning of our revelation of the kingdom of Babylon around us the influence of it in our daily lives was revealed. We have begun to cut away the tangled undergrowth on the ancient path, which impaired our view, by recognizing the cleverly disguised "celebrations" of Satan's taking the place of our Father's ordained festivals.

For us to think that this is all, limits the greatness and sovereignty of YHWH; for this is only the beginning. There is still more to pull down to be able to return to the old ways of the Elohim of creation.

As clay in the hands of the potter, we cannot afford to become stiff and un-moldable. We must allow Him to continue to fashion us into a vessel to show forth His glory.

As I have torn out the crab grass in front of me, I have noticed that the path has been narrowing. With each "section" cleared, less have come along side me to continue the walk; not necessarily that there isn't room – it's just too scary or difficult to pull up those particular "attractive" weeds.

If we truly want to pursue Him in all areas of life then we must be willing to examine every "plant" we encounter. We need to ask: "Is that really His plant on the path, or has it just been there so long it feels normal to have it there?" Be willing to ask: "What is **His** normal?"

I would like to give evidence for you to examine the calendar we now fashion our days by and the original created calendar YHWH set up at the beginning of time.

I would ask you to be pliable in the hands of our loving Father as He continues to awaken the bones of His people and bring the two sticks – the whole house of Israel - together in His hand. Our Father has asked us to have no other god before Him and to remember the Sabbath and keep it set apart.

I ask you: Is **His** Sabbath relevant? According to

what He has to say about it in His Word, I would say it is very relevant. It is the sign between Him and us His people.

   Shouldn't we make sure we are keeping His Sabbath and Feasts the way they were originally placed on His calendar and not the one molded to fit this world we live in?

   The first part of Jeremiah 6:16 says: *Thus saith Yahweh, Stand ye in the ways, and see, **and ask for the old paths**, where is the good way, and walk therein, and ye shall find rest for your souls....*

   This is what He wants of us. Let us not fit the last part of this scripture: *But they said, 'We will not walk in it.'*

Shalom, Diane

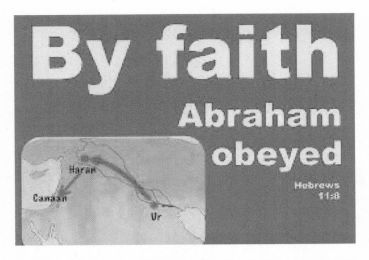

JEWISH? NOPE, HEBREW!
(DEFINING WORDS)

It is my concern that some words used in this book will not be understood by some people because they seem to be Jewish, so I felt a chapter on these specific words and the origin would be helpful. After years of studying and researching Hebrew meanings of certain words, I realized I might be 'leaving some people in the dust' who weren't familiar with the Hebrew language.

First let us start with the identification of these words. To be labeled 'Jewish" is incorrect. The word "Jewish" was placed upon the surviving Hebrews who came back from exile. The people who went into captivity in Babylon at the time of Nebuchadnezzar were from the southern kingdom of Israel whose dominant tribe was Judah; hence the title 'house of Judah'. To be 'Jewish' is to be of the house of Judah. The northern kingdom of Israel, which consisted of 10 of the 12 tribes, was defeated and absorbed by the Assyrians before Judah went to Babylon. The northern tribes were known by two different names; Ephraim (which was the dominant tribe) and Israel. When Judah came back to the land they also took on the full name of Israel for they were what was left of the whole house of Israel.

Now, let us look at what the Hebrew language is. First of all, the 'Hebrew" language is considered the original tongue of mankind. It is also known as a Semitic language. What, you may ask is Semitic? Let's go back to the flood. Noah had three sons. Japheth, Shem and Ham. It is the line of Shem that God used to eventually produce our Messiah. The tongue which came down from Shem is – Semitic. The Semitic language is also very close to Aramaic (Arabian) and Assyrian (Iran, Iraq, Babylon), which have some variances in the root words. If you would take some time researching the lineage of Noah's sons, you would see where the 'Shemites" lived. The reason we call the tongue of Israel "Hebrew", is because Abraham came from Ur and 'crossed over' to the land of Canaan and followed YHWH. The word for cross over is 'eber' or – Hebrew. It is also the name of one of the ancestors of Abraham which was Eber and Abraham was the first called a Hebrew - עברי 'ibrîy ib-ree' (Patronymic from H5677; an Eberite (that is, Hebrew) or descendant of Eber – Hebrew) - (Genesis 14:13). Because of this bloodline being the chosen line, the words we read every day in His book were originally written in Hebrew. In fact, there is a verse Zephaniah 3:8 that uses all the letters of the Hebrew alphabet including the final forms called the sopheet form of which there are five of them, and then goes on to say in the next verse: *Zep 3:9 "For then I will restore to the peoples **a pure language,** That they all may call on the name of the LORD, To serve Him with one accord.* Is that a coincidence? I don't think so. Sometimes to get the proper meaning of something in scripture, it is advantageous to go back to the original language. This is what I have done and why there is "Hebrew" in the book.

Let me now take you through what I have written in the book:

YHWH, YHVH, or יהוה - These three sets of letters or symbols are the proper name for God Almighty, the great I AM. Every place you see LORD or GOD all in caps, the third set of symbols above is what is written in the Hebrew. I use the English ones when referring to His true name. This word will also appear as "Yahweh". What you need to understand is that the LORD is a title, not a proper name. It would be like someone always calling you "the wife" or "the husband" or "the baker".

ELOHIM - This word always appears as 'God' in our bibles. However, Elohim has a more full meaning. The word 'Elohim' is plural – Think on that a minute. It is all encompassing the Elohim we serve. Father, Word, Spirit (Ruach, which is the breath or wind) in one word.

YESHUA- or **YEHOSHUA**- -The proper name of Jesus. Meaning - *Jehovah-saved*; (Matt 1:21). Whenever you see 'Jesus' written in the New

Testament, if you look it up in the Greek, you will see this:

Ἰησοῦς   *Iēsous*   *ee-ay-sooce'*

*Of Hebrew origin [H3091]; Jesus **(that is, Jehoshua)**, the name of our Lord and two (three) other Israelites: - Jesus.*

What is interesting, is the Hebrew number in the Old Testament that they refer to – H3091. If you look at that one in the Strong's you will see this:

yeh-ho-shoo'-ah,   yᵉhôshûa
*From H3068 and H3467; **Jehovah-saved**; Jehoshua (that is, Joshua), the Jewish leader: - Jehoshua, Jehoshuah, Joshua.*

Now here I must ask the question – why did the translators use 'Jesus' instead of Joshua as they did in the Old Testament? Using 'Jesus' actually hides the *meaning* of His name. Reading the account in Mathew 1:21 *"And she will bring forth a Son, and you shall call His name Jesus, for **He will save** His people from their sins."* And then you look at the meaning of 'yehoshua' or 'Joshua' – it means just that.

TORAH – This word has been translated as "law", however it means something much more in Hebrew. It means **teachings and instructions**: The direction one is to take in life.

It also is the word identifying the first five books of the Bible.

SHALOM – This too has special meaning. We take it to mean 'peace', and it does, however it means more. It means completeness:

שָׁלֹם שׁלם (shâlôm) (*shaw-lome'*) ; *safe*, that is, (figuratively) *well, happy, friendly*; also (abstractly) *welfare*, that is, health, prosperity, peace: - X do, familiar, X fare, favour, + friend, X greet, (good) health, (X perfect, such as be at) peace (-able, -ably), prosper (-ity, -ous), rest, safe (-ly), salute, welfare, (X all is, be) well, X wholly.

KADOSH – This word is the word HOLY in English. This too is a more descriptive word in Hebrew. It means **Set apart:** Someone or something that has been separated from the rest for a special purpose.

MOED – This is the Hebrew word used when referring to an **appointment of YHWH**. It will appear as 'Feasts', 'appointed times', solemn feasts, or tabernacle of congregation in our English bibles.

HAG – (or chag) -This is a special word used for three of the feasts of YHWH that were to be held in Jerusalem. It is translated as **'feast'**, which can get confusing if you do not look at it in the original Hebrew language to differentiate which kind of feast they are to do.

חקה, khook-kaw' - Throughout the book you will see groups like this. Hebrew letters first then English pronunciation and then a description. I have done this to show a word that needs to be seen for what it is, not just what the English word says.

SHABBATH/SABBATH - This word means simply: **Ceasing:** A stopping of work activity. Often used for the seventh day or special feast day as a day set aside for resting or celebrating.

YOM TERUAH, YOM KIPPUR, SUKKOT - These three words are the Hebrew names for the three feasts in the 7th month on the Hebrew calendar. They are in plain English – Day of Trumpets, Day of Atonement, and Tabernacles. One thing interesting with the second word is that in Leviticus 23 the word is in the plural form – **KIPPURIM** – atonements. The third word is basically "tents".

SHAVUOT - You would recognize this feast more as Pentecost. However, Pentecost means 'fiftieth', Whereas Shavuot means 'weeks'.

RABBI SHLOMO YITZCHAKI (RASHI) - Rashi was a prominent Rabbi whose commentaries on the scriptures where very much revered. One who quoted Rashi, quoted a well-respected viewpoint.

JASHER - Many have misunderstood Jasher to be a person who authored the book by that name. This is incorrect.

יׁשׁר   yâshâr   *yaw-shawr'*
A tight rope or cord is straight. *A righteous one is one who is straight and firmly holds up truth* just as the cord is straight and firmly holds the wall of the tent upright.

This is a book written by upright men through the ages until the time of the judges. The responsibility to record historical things was handed down from generation to generation to one who was upright and true to write the happenings from the time of Adam to the Judges. The true title of this book is - "the book of the upright," or "the upright or correct record."

MISHNA - This is a collection of notes taken during many discussions on the scriptures. They were compiled into a written collection after 200CE called the Talmud.

TALMUD - The Talmud was the "oral law" which was all the teachings of the "sages" consisting of comments on the text of the Bible.

R. Jehudah the Nasi, was the compiler of the Mishna. With the help of his many friends and sympathizers he was finally enabled to arrange in order six sections of Mishnayoth, condensed from hundreds. Each section is given up to a general subject, and is subdivided into tracts dealing with matters which come naturally within the scope of the section, The tracts are further divided into chapters. From these emerged the final compilation of the written Talmud.

I hope that these explanations will help you in understanding what I am saying while reading this book.

YOU WANT ANSWERS?

There is a movie from the 90's titled: A Few Good Men. In this film is a scene with a witness and a lawyer. The dialogue goes like this:

Witness: "You want answers?" Lawyer: "I want the truth!" Witness: "You can't handle the truth!"

With that verbal exchange in mind – just how much truth can you handle?

1. The Roman (Julian, Gregorian) calendar is **NOT** YHWH's calendar. It is pagan.

2. YHWH gave us only 1 calendar not 2 and it is based on the sun, moon and stars (Gen. 1:14).

3. ALL His appointed times are on HIS calendar.

4. Using the Roman calendar to determine ANY of YHWH's appointed times is mixing with pagan practices.

5. The present Jewish calendar has been corrupted since the destruction of the Temple.

6. The time frame of the calendar metamorphous was during the 2nd to 4th century.

7. Because of the mixing of two calendars, 'band aids' have been put on the Jewish calendar to try to fix the discrepancies of clashing feasts (i.e. Day of Atonement and the Sabbath day) such as rules of postponements, delaying new moon, establishing fences and ignoring the actual sighting of the sliver of the moon.

8. YHWH's day does NOT start at the beginning of darkness. He called the LIGHT good (Gen.1:4). Never does He call darkness good. Day is continuously spoken of before night in scripture.

9. The beginning of the month is determined by the appearance of the new sliver of the moon the evening before; not the astrological molad of conjunction (dark moon).

10. Following a constant Saturday Sabbath appears simple; however, it becomes complicated when it collides with the instructions in scripture in following the Feasts. Once you understand YHWH's calendar it remains simple.

11. Determining the day of the Hebrews Sabbath in BC and 1st century AD using a pagan Roman historian who hated Jews in the 2nd and 3rd century AD and who knew Saturnday was the first day of the week, is like determining the day Yeshua was crucified by going back in time with the modern Roman Gregorian calendar; which by the way is pagan and not created until the 16th century AD.

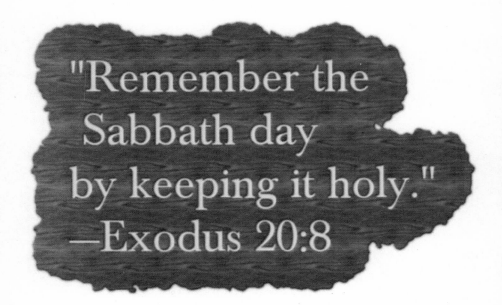

"Remember the
Sabbath day
by keeping it holy."
—Exodus 20:8

WHEN IS YHWH'S SABBATH?

In many of the sources I have read, there was an
element of evolutional thinking in the progress of man.
Ancient man was looked upon as underdeveloped,
superstitious and ignorant. How arrogant we have
become. I believe **we** are the ignorant ones. We
have been duped through the generations that we
know it all - We have ascended to heights way above
our ancestors in knowledge - when really we know
less than they did. Can any of us rattle off the
constellations and explain *why* they are up there?
Do we know how the sun and moon work together to
point out the month and season we are in and follow
them through each mansion? Do we understand the
positions and phases of the moon and *why* they even
happen? Without this information we cannot know His
true appointed times. It is readily the argument of
many that the creation account is the model of the
seven day week we now observe in perpetual

procession and has always been that way from the beginning of time- **but, has it**?. I agree that Father has given us the pattern of 6 days work and 7th rest. However, I think if you would allow yourself to look at the lunar/solar calendar (or the true created calendar; the biblical calendar), it is in that very pattern. It is also in a place that man cannot tamper with it - **in the heavens**.

Let us take a moment to read a few verses from the scriptures that may show you the intentions of the Father in the keeping of His appointed times:

Jer 31:35 *Thus said יהוה, who gives the sun for a light by day, **and the laws of the moon and the stars** for a light by night, who stirs up the sea, and its waves roar – יהוה of hosts is His Name.* What laws are these? The word in Hebrew here is:

H2708 - *חקה, khook-kaw' Feminine of H2706, and meaning substantially the same: - appointed, custom, manner, ordinance, site, statute.*

H2706 - *חק, khoke From H2710; an enactment; hence an appointment (of time, space, quantity, labor or usage): - appointed, bound, commandment, convenient, custom, decree (-d), due, law, measure, X necessary, ordinance (-nary), portion, set time, statute, task.*

H2710 - *חקק, khaw-kak' A primitive root; properly to hack, that is, engrave; by implication to enact (laws being cut in stone or metal tablets in primitive times) or (generally) prescribe: - appoint, decree, governor,*

27

grave, lawgiver, note, portray, print, set.

Apparently this is a law that has been engraved upon the moon. What was engraved? An *enactment*; hence an *appointment* (of time, space, quantity, labor or usage). Where or when was this done?

*Gen 1:14 And Elohim said, "Let lights come to be in the expanse of the heavens **to separate the day from the night, and let them be for signs and appointed times, and for days and years**, 15 and let them be for lights in the expanse of the heavens **to give light on the earth.**" And it came to be so. 16 And Elohim made two great lights: the greater light to rule the day, and the lesser light to rule the night, and the stars. 17 And Elohim set them in the expanse of the heavens to give light on the earth, 18 and **to rule** over the day and over the night, and **to separate** the light from the darkness. And Elohim saw that it was good. 19 And there came to be evening and there came to be morning, **the fourth day**.*

This verse is more significant than we think. These lights were set in motion on the **fourth day** of creation. Bear with me as I walk through the mystery design of Father's Menorah. The Menorah, which was designed by YHWH, is made up of seven candlesticks. Three branches out on each side of the middle candlestick. Each one can represent the "sevens" of God; seven spirits, seven creation days, seven feasts, seven churches, seven trumpets, seven seals, seven bowls, etc. At this time I would like to focus on the middle candlestick, which is the 4th candlestick. This candlestick stands for the servant Spirit of God. It is considered the "hinge" or center for the other 6 candlesticks. It represents Yeshua, who is the Word of YHWH made flesh– in whom all creation turns or centers on. It is also the place of the fourth letter of the Hebrew alphabet – the *dalet*. This is, in ancient Hebrew symbols, a door. So, we know that He (the Word) - is the door. All things depend on Yeshua (the Word) and turn or pivot on Him. Now compare this information with the fourth day of creation; the sun, moon and stars. Could they possibly be the signs that all time pivots or centers on? Isn't it interesting that this would be the very day that our Father spoke and set His time piece in place?

As we examine statements from various sources, we may encounter things that are not in total agreement or harmony with each writer, like - how you figure the week on a lunar based calendar or when did men begin to pull away from this certain way of following the days? Try to keep in mind the **example** of a report from a group of archaeologists that have examined some ancient bones just unearthed as you read on. They all have their input as to what possibly happened. Some may say it died violently. Others may say it died of old age. Some may say it was a meat eater and yet others may say it ate herbs. *They all agree the skeleton is there*, they just have different ideas of what took place.

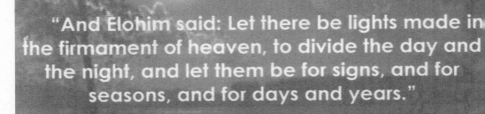

"And Elohim said: Let there be lights made in the firmament of heaven, to divide the day and the night, and let them be for signs, and for seasons, and for days and years."

- Genesis1:14

A CALENDAR BY ANY OTHER NAME

I find it very interesting that we here and now know very little about calendar history. First off -----which calendar is it that matters to us? Which calendar tells us the story of the past? Which calendar do we 'hang our hat on' for true reference of events?

I guess a good time in history to begin is right after the Messiah. This time is what matters to us as to how we should keep His Passover, Unleavened Bread, First Fruits, Shavuot (Feast of Weeks), Day of Trumpets, Day of Atonement, Tabernacles and His Sabbath.

Hardly anyone has ever carefully examined exactly when these feasts are to be done.

As I started digging for information on the calendar, I found some very interesting things. First I started with the Gregorian (present day) calendar. This calendar did not come into existence until the 16th century. So, I went back to the Julian calendar (created by Julius Caesar) which was the predecessor of the Gregorian. This calendar did quite a metamorphosis in its lifetime. To start with; the Roman calendar was a lunar calendar believed to have been started by Romulus in 735 BC. This calendar had an 8-day week called the Nundina. The 8th day was the market day. Each year the letter indicating that day would change according to where it landed in the beginning of the new year. In 46 BC, after visiting Cleopatra (Pharaoh of Egypt at that time), Julius Caesar reformed the calendar to a solar calendar which was fashioned after the one used in Egypt. The Egyptian calendar however, broke the month up into 3 'weeks' of 10 days. The Julian calendar was at first mixed with the old lunar figuring, because the titles of Kalends (*beginning of month*), Nones (*end of month*), and Ides (*middle of month*) were still used and there were still 8 days a week. The nundinal cycle was eventually replaced by the seven-day week where each day was named for a Roman god and **began with the day of Saturn**. This first came into use in Italy during the early Roman imperial period in the 2nd century (100–199 CE). The system of nundinal letters was also adapted for the week. For a while, the week and the nundinal cycle coexisted, but by the time the week was officially adopted by Constantine in AD 321 (4th century), the nundinal cycle had fallen out of use and the day of the Sun took the place of first day and Saturn was bumped to last.

During the 2nd and 3rd centuries (100AD – 299AD) this Roman mess was being followed. In that same area there were other calendars being used. From reading several writings of different historical persons, I discovered at least the following calendars: Egyptian, Macedonian, Hebrew, and Roman were used. These were all going on at the same time. To say the least, having all these calendars being observed in the same area at approximately the same time, it was not an easy thing to coordinate the feast date unless you were following the Hebrew calendar. The one feast that steered the course of the Gentile believers' church away from the Jewish believers' church was the date of the Passover observance. While the Bishops of the circumcision (Jewish believers) were stationed in Jerusalem, the proper observances of YHWH's feasts were being upheld. However, in 135 AD (2nd century) Hadrian laid siege on Jerusalem and changed the lives of the Jews drastically. He forbid the Torah and stopped the Hebrew calendar. He then banished all Jews from the city and surrounding area even to the point of not being able to gaze at it. With the Bishops of the circumcision removed, the gentile believers stepped into the church leadership role in the Jerusalem area. Without Hebrew influence to stay on track according to the correct calendar (Hebrew luni\solar), followers of Yeshua began to drift away from observing the proper appointed feasts. It was also at this time that much upheaval with the orthodox Jews and their calendar observances was taking place. Because of the persecution towards the Jews, there were compromises being performed by the leadership of especially the Babylonian Jews. They were willing to "adjust" their way of life and standards – **even to the changing of their Sabbaths** – to fit in more and relieve the pressure of persecution.

While digging for some kind of path that was carved at this time, I realized that this was such a time of turmoil for not just Jews and Christians, but for all who lived in the area. As one writer said – This was a time when they were busier with speaking life than recording it (my paraphrase).

What was the possible way the early Hebrews kept track of all the Feasts of YHWH? What kind of calendar did they go by? Obviously it was not the Roman one for they were forced to use it or any other one in use at the time of Hadrian, since he forbade them to use theirs. What does history say? What do the old writings of other researchers of the past say?

I have copied two quotes from my list of research pages. To read all the different sources I have found, go to the section titled "JUST GIVE ME THE FACTS, PLEASE" towards the end of this book.

HERSCHEL SHANKS

Biblical Archaeology Society

"There were very marked differences, in the attitude toward government and the preservation of Jewish religion and life, between the Palestinian and Babylonian Jews. The Palestinian Jews jealously guarded their religion and way of life, while the Babylonian Jews were clearly, willing to accommodate the government of their area and

*compromise certain principles they held. **This included the Sabbath day.** During this time, a major revival of the Zoroastrian religion, took place in (226 A.D.), when the first Sassanian king, Ardeshir, came to the Persian throne. He made reforms to the old lunar-based calendar, which had a far-reaching effect on his people, (especially the Jews), who initially rejected his new calendar, since it affected their religious observances. This resulted, for a while, in two calendars, one decreed by the king and the other, older one, followed by the majority of the people in the kingdom. Eventually, however, the new calendar won out and the Persians, as well as the Jews of Babylonia, **began to organize their sabbaths, according to the new solar calendar."***

JAMES DWYER

"ADVANCED ASTRONOMY IN BIBLE TEXTS", & "A NEW LOOK AT THE CHRISTIAN SABBATH"

*"The Early Christian descriptions of a weekly cycle containing periodic single days are very clear, and this information (coupled with evidence provided by the measurable lunar/solar phenomena) **strongly indicates that Early Christians were practicing a lunar-based calendar".***

*"It now seems almost certain that some additional definitions of the early Sabbath cycle are missing from the modern tradition of the seven-day week. Essentially, **the modern week**, as a continuous cycle of seven days, **does not seem to equate to the definition of the week as it was used during the Early Christian era."***

*"This new research looks at the Sabbath calendar, as it would have been known to a mainstream Jew, **living in the second temple era, and it finds the Sabbath to have been a***

rather sophisticated interface with the lunar-solar system.
*In this earlier time, the Sabbath cycle, surprisingly, **was***
***defined by the phases of the moon,** and, even more*
*surprising than this, the **Sabbath cycle also revolved into***
precise alignment with the Annual Feast Circuit".

Days	1	2	3	4	5	6	7
			WORK				Refreshed REST
Years	1000	2000	3000	4000	5000	6000	7000
			WORK				REST Refreshing

WHAT DOES YHWH MEAN BY 6 DAYS WORK, THE 7TH REST?

I would like to start this next section with the first Feast of YHWH. I guess this is one of the most confusion causing commands that is given by YHWH. I have prayed and pondered and asked about this statement for as long as I can remember while walking this road of obedience to the Torah.

Luk 11:9 So I say to you: Keep asking, and it will be given you. Keep searching, and you will find. Keep knocking, and the door will be opened for you.

This is a very true and comforting statement by Yeshua. For Father, I believe, showed me the meaning for His statement:

Exo 20:9 Six days you shall labor, and do all your work. 10 But on the seventh day is the Sabbath of YHWH your Elohim; on it you shall do no work: you, nor your son, nor your daughter, your servant nor your maidservant, your ox, nor your donkey, nor any cattle of yours, nor the stranger that sojourns with you.

Seven times this commandment is made in the 5 books of Moses. Seven.......the number of YHWH.

I believe we have missed what He was telling us in this. It is not saying "I want you to count a continuous stream of days – 6 days - 7th, 6 days - 7th, 6 days - 7th." He is giving us the perfect (or tamim) 'Sabbath week' as the first Feast to remember; for it comes the most often. It comes 4 times a month. Now the question to ask at this time is what is a month to YHWH? There are in Hebrew two words that are interchangeable for meaning a cycle of around 30 days. Those two are moon and month – xry-yerach, sdx-hodesh. Yerach can be translated moon or month and hodesh can be translated month or new moon. Let's examine this a little further. A perfect set of verses to show the use of both words is in I kings 6:37-38:

*In the fourth year hath the house of Jehovah been founded, in the **month** Zif, and in the eleventh year, in the **month** Bul-- that is the eighth **month**--hath the house been finished in all its matters, and in all its ordinances, and he buildeth it seven years.*

The first two times it says 'month'; it is the word yerach. The last 'month' is hodesh. So, what it is really saying is: In the 'lunation period' of Zif,…in the 'lunation period' of Bul—that is the eighth New Moon.

What you are reading here is that YHWH's calendar is based on the moon lunation period of 29 to 30 days and is marked with the New Moon as the start of the month - or lunation period. Look at each command when to start each Feast of YHWH. It is based on a day in the month of the lunation period. Not the Roman calendar (Julian or Gregorian).

If our Father has placed all of His appointed times by the days of the lunar month, why wouldn't He also place the important appointed time of the Sabbath in the same way? Do we serve an Elohim of confusion or of order?

How, you may ask, do you know this "Sabbath Week" is correct? I will ask you; can you explain why there is so much confusion in the counting of the omer time? Some start the count on the 16th, which is the proper First Fruits day, but some start the count the day after the *Saturday* Sabbath; which could be more days away from the 16th. Many times this count is started right after a day called the 'high Sabbath'. So what do you do? Count 7 **high** Sabbaths and then add the fiftieth day? Where is that in Torah? However, if you follow Father's perfect 'Sabbath week' you will have no problem with the count.

*Lev 23:11 And he shall wave the sheaf before the LORD, to be accepted for you; **on the morrow after the Sabbath the priest shall wave it.***

Lev 23:15 `And ye have numbered to you from the morrow of the sabbath, from the day of your bringing in the sheaf of the wave-offering: they are seven perfect sabbaths; 16 unto the morrow of the seventh sabbath ye do number fifty days, and ye have brought near a new present to Jehovah;

Here right in Leviticus it talks of perfect Sabbaths. This means 'undefiled'. How do you NOT defile a Sabbath in the counting? **Make sure you count only the perfect 'Sabbath week' – 6 days in succession of work and the 7th rest (Sabbath).**

Throughout scripture it is understood that New Moon Day is not one of the 6 work days or a Sabbath. These two days are always mentioned separate.

*Eze 46:1 Thus saith the Master YHVH; The gate of the inner court that looks toward the east **shall be shut the six working days; but on the sabbath it shall be opened**, and **in the day of the new moon it shall be opened.***

The only way to count perfect Sabbath weeks is by YHWH's perfect calendar of using the moon to count the days by its lunation cycle starting with new moon day and **then dividing into 4 perfect (or undefiled) Sabbath weeks**. Every special day of YHWH is tied to the **moonth!**

To read all my research on this subject, again see "*JUST GIVE ME THE FACTS PLEASE*" at the end.

S
H
A
V
U
O
T

SHAVUOT OR PENTECOST

If you do not understand the true title for Shavuot (Feast of Weeks) and what it is portraying, you will not comprehend the true counting to Pentecost (fiftieth) day. Why is it called Feast of **WEEKS**? Obviously there is a specific reason for it. It is not called the Feast of counting fifty days, so, why do people do it that way?

Lev 23:11 And he shall wave the sheaf before YHVH, to be accepted for you: on the morrow after the sabbath the priest shall wave it.12 And ye shall offer that day when ye wave the sheaf an he lamb without blemish of the first year for a burnt offering unto YHVH.13 And the meat offering thereof shall be two tenth deals of fine flour mingled with oil, an offering made by fire unto YHVH for a sweet savour: and the drink offering thereof shall be of wine, the fourth part of an hin.14 And ye shall eat neither bread, nor parched corn, nor green ears, until the selfsame day that ye have brought an offering unto your Elohim: it shall be a statute for ever throughout your generations in all your dwellings.15 And ye shall count unto you from the morrow after the sabbath, from the day that ye brought the sheaf of the wave offering; seven sabbaths shall be complete 16 Even unto the morrow after the seventh sabbath shall ye number fifty days; and ye shall offer a new meat offering unto YHVH.

In verse 15, you will see the word 'complete'. This word in the Hebrew language is – תמים   tâmîym. It means undefiled, perfect, without blemish, entire.....

Num 28:26 Also in the day of the firstfruits, when ye bring a new meat offering unto YHVH, after your weeks be out, ye shall have an holy convocation; ye shall do no servile work:

Deu 16:9 Seven weeks shalt thou number unto thee: **begin to number the seven weeks** *from such time as thou beginnest to put the sickle to the corn.10 **And thou shalt keep the feast of weeks unto YHVH thy Elohim** with a tribute of a freewill offering of thine hand, which thou shalt give unto YHVH thy Elohim, according as YHVH thy Elohim hath blessed thee:*

Notice that Moses says "seven weeks" in Deuteronomy. He had to have understood the concept of a perfect Sabbath week to associate his instructions with the instructions of YHWH in Leviticus 23 and Numbers 28. Why would YHWH emphasize the counting of **7 Sabbaths complete** (perfect or undefiled) – 7 Sabbaths plus one more day after the 7th Sabbath (49+1=50), instead of just telling us to count 50 days in succession? What is He telling us about this Feast and its timing? Could we possibly mess up the right time to observe this day? If we do not stay on YHWH's calendar, we could! How amazing it is that our Father has preserved His calendar for us by these simple instructions, for the only way to accomplish what He has set for us to do here is on His calendar – not the Roman one. To count 7 Sabbaths **undefiled** can only be done with the **perfect Sabbath week** (6 days work - in succession - and then the Sabbath). Remember, New Moon day is not counted as a work day or a Sabbath, so is not included in the perfect Sabbath week count. Nor is the extra 30th day of some of the months counted for it stands alone separate from the other work days.

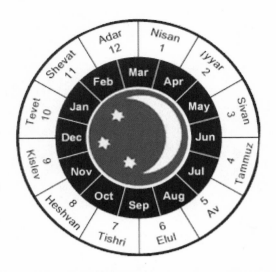

CAN YOU PLEASE EXPLAIN HOW YHWH'S CALENDAR WORKS?

Many of you who have only the western Roman calendar (Gregorian) to look to for setting dates and following holidays, the following calendar may seem a bit strange. However it is the original way days, months, feasts, weeks, and fasts were kept track of by the children of YHWH from the beginning of time until, I believe, the 2nd or 3rd century A.D..   Okay, let's begin.

YHWH created the sun to give us daylight to work and to count off - along with the star constellations - a full year. He created the moon for the determining of the months by counting off the days (by the changing of the phases each time it appears) for a period of 29 to 30 days from the appearing to the reappearing sliver. At the appearing of the first visible sliver of the moon at evening, out of Israel (the land); the next morning the new month is set for the fresh counting. When determining the calendar's days with the Sabbath included, we must look at scripture. Things need to harmonize with it. In Scripture the New Moon and Sabbath are always talked about separately. This shows that New Moon Day is never the Sabbath. There is only one New Moon Day that is treated like a Sabbath and that is Day of Trumpets. New Moon Day is also not considered one of the 6 work days of the Sabbath week (**Eze 46:1**). So, what is it? **It is the signal** for the beginning of a new month. It is the first day of the month but not the first day of the 6 work days. The count for the first work day begins the day *after* New Moon Day. YHWH established this perfect 'Sabbath week' for us to keep things straight when He would ask us to count *7 Sabbaths perfect* to Shavuot. The count begins the day after the Sabbath (or 15th of Nissan) which is the 16th or *"first day of the week"* and ends the day after the 7th Sabbath. During this counting, we cross over to a new month twice. That is why we are told to count only the 'undefiled' Sabbaths – or *perfect* 'Sabbath week' (6 days work 7th day rest). 7 perfect Sabbath weeks = 49 days plus one more day after the 7th Sabbath =50. None of us have ever understood why YHWH kept reiterating the 6 days work and 7th rest. We were told it was because YHWH created the week separate from the rest of His calendar. I believe the Word says He is not an Elohim of confusion – doesn't it? In believing the week runs totally independent of the most intricate time piece ever made makes no sense. Things don't fit together in harmony and some things run into each other! That my friend is confusion!

Let's start laying out the calendar with the information we have at this time. We will use the 7th Lunar Month called Tishri. I will place the Gregorian days on calendar so you can see how it fits. The Lunar numbers are on left top corner and the Gregorian numbers are bottom right.

SEVENTH MONTH – TISHRI   2014

SUNDAY	MONDAY	TUESDAY	WEDNESDAY	THURSDAY	FRIDAY	SATURDAY
					Moon sighted	1 New Moon
			Sep 24	25	26	27
2 Workday	3 Workday	4 Workday	5 Workday	6 Workday	7 Workday	8 SABBATH
28	29	30	Oct 1	2	3	4
9	10	11	12	13	14	15 SABBATH
5	6	7	8	9	10	TABERNACLES 1
16	17	18	19	20	21	22 SABBATH
2	3	4	5	6	7	SIMCHAT TORAH
23	24	25	26	27	28	29 SABBATH
19	20	21	22	23	24	25

Remember what I said earlier, New Moon day is NOT a Sabbath. According to scripture it was a day of worship, but there is no restriction to work (Exodus 40:2). The new sliver of the moon was sighted in Israel on the night of Friday the 26th of September, which means the next morning begins the new month, which is New Moon Day. Now, if New Moon DAY signals the beginning of a new month then you can actually overlay the Gregorian calendar, and the next 4 *Gregorian* Saturdays will be the lunar Sabbath day. New Moon Day is the first counted day of the **new month** but, because it is not a Sabbath or a work day, **the next day** starts the count of the 6 working days. You may ask: How does this help in counting to Shavuot? Haven't you ever wondered why YHWH Says 7 Sabbaths complete? Why didn't He just say count 50 days starting with the 16th of Nissan? Why did He say start the count after the *Sabbath?* We know from scripture that Yeshua was hung on the tree on the day of the 14th of Nissan *(Passover)* and was put in the tomb that night. It said that the women saw where He was laid and went home for the Sabbath was coming. That would make the 15th a Sabbath. All Jewish writings show the 16th the day of First Fruits and the day to start the count. That would be according to YHWH's instructions *'the morrow after (of) the Sabbath'.* Let us now look at the count of the 7 Sabbaths **PERFECT.**

1st Lunar Month · ABIB (NISSAN) · 2014

Sun.	Mon.	Tues.	Wed	Thurs.	Fri	Sat
	14	15	16	17	18	19
	Passover	Sabbath	First Fruits 1	2	3	4
20	21	22	23	24	25	26
5	6	7 (1st Sab)	8	9	10	11
27	28	29	30			
12	13	14 (2nd Sab)	moon sighted			

2nd Lunar Month · IYAR · 2014

Sun	Mon	Tues	Wed	Thurs	Fri	Sat
				1	2	3
				New Moon	15	16
4	5	6	7	8	9	10
17	18	19	20	21 (3rd Sab)	22	23
11	12	13	14	15	16	17
24	25	26	27	28 (4th Sab)	29	30
18	19	20	21	22	23	24
31	32	33	34	35 (5th Sab)	36	37
25	26	27	28	29	30	
38	39	40	41	42 (6th Sab)	moon sighted	

3rd Lunar Month · SIVAN · 2014

Sun	Mon	Tues	Wed	Thurs	Fri	Sat
						1
						New Moon
2	3	4	5	6	7	8
43	44	45	46	47	48	49 (7th Sab)
9						
50 PENTECOST						

48

You can see on page 48 the 7 undefiled weeks are in the different shaded lines (6 work days plus a Sabbath) and placed on the modern day calendar for a familiar background. Notice I have not put any Gregorian dates on these, just the lunar dates. You will notice that both Abib and Iyar had the extra 30th day added to their months in the year of 2014. The 30th is **not connected** to a perfect Sabbath week so it was not counted as one of the omer days, as New Moon Day also was not counted. We are counting only the perfect Sabbath week of 7 days.

When following YHWH's proper calendar according to His sun, moon and stars His feasts lay neatly into place with no extra "high" Sabbaths to confuse matters. Also, Yom Kippur **never** lands on the Sabbath. There is never the question "do we fast or feast?" *Father keeps His fasts separate from His feasts.*

YHWH wants us to be set apart from the world. He has also instructed us to not worship the heavens like the pagans who followed the phases of first quarter, full, and last quarter of the moon. He has not connected His Sabbaths or yearly feasts to the exact phases of the moon. We are to *count the days from New Moon Day which is the morning after the first sighting of the moon* – nothing else. I believe this is the way it was done from the beginning. There are many statements of this in historical writings and encyclopedias. See the reference pages titled *"JUST GIVE ME THE FACTS PLEASE"* at end of this book.

BEHOLD, THE MOON

When I became aware of the verse written in Jeremiah 31:35, I decided to observe the moon as much as I could to try to understand in any small way just what was assigned to it. I began to watch every new moon that was visible and discovered something interesting.

Did you know that the moon's illumination changes shape every day?

Did you know that the moon's illumination "rocks" through the year?

Did you know that this rocking tells you when you are approaching the beginning of the appointed first month of YHWH's calendar?

Did you know that each new moon sliver is a different size?

Did you know that by seeing that sliver size generally tells you if it is to be a 29 or 30 day month?

Did you know that the moon rises about 50 minutes later each day?

Did you know the moon follows the sun in its waxing and precedes the sun in its waning?

Did you know that because the change of the speed in the moon's course over the face of the earth can vary by 13.4 hours each month no one really knows the day or the hour of the actual conjunction of the sun and moon?

Did you know that at the conjunction (dark time) of the moon with the sun, the moon can be hidden in the Middle East (Israel) from 1.5 days to almost 3.5 days?

The scriptures are full of the marveling of YHWH's sovereign placement of the sun, moon and stars and the assigning of their duties and the covenant He has with them. How could we possibly think we know the purpose of the moon or its importance? Who are we to turn our eyes to a manmade calendar with calculated mathematical new moons instead of beholding the majesty of His creation and seeing the heavens declare His glory? Why do we down play their role in His creation? Again, I reiterate:

*Gen 1:14 And Elohim said, "**Let lights** come to be in the expanse of the heavens to separate the day from the night, and **let them be for signs** and appointed times, and for days and years, 15 and **let them be for lights** in the expanse of the heavens **to give light** on the earth." And it came to be so. 16 And Elohim **made two great lights:** the greater light to rule the day, and the lesser **light to rule the night**, and the stars. 17 And Elohim set them in the expanse of the heavens **to give light** on the earth, 18 and **to rule over** the day and over **the night**, and **to separate the light from the darkness.** And Elohim saw that it was good*

*Deu 4:19 and lest you lift up your eyes to the heavens, and shall **see** the sun, and the moon, and the stars – all the host of the heavens – and you be drawn away into bowing down to them and serving them, which יהוה your Elohim **has allotted to all the peoples under all the heavens.***

*Psa 8:3 For I see Your heavens, the work of Your fingers, The moon and the stars, **which You have established.***

*Psa 89:37 "Like the moon, it is established forever, And **the witness in the heaven** is steadfast." Selah.*

*Psa 104:19 **He made the moon for appointed times;** The sun knows its going down.*

NEW MOON DAY
CONCEALED, FULL, OR CRESCENT
THAT IS THE QUESTION!

After seeing the extraordinary aspects of the moon itself, let us examine the three different beliefs of **when** New Moon day is. We will bring in historical documents for each one and compare the information, then we will examine **what** New Moon Day is. Let us begin with the concealed moon.

Concealed Moon

In modern language the term "New Moon" refers to that little black dot on our calendars today. Modern astronomers adopted the name "New Moon" which is when the moon is in its dark phase and is not visible. There are now two ways the "New Moon" is recognized; the *"astronomical"* New Moon and the *"crescent"* New Moon. "Astronomical" New Moon means New Moon as used by the astronomers, i.e. conjunction or dark, and "crescent" New Moon is used in the original meaning of the first visible sliver. Some people have sought Biblical support for this modern meaning of New Moon. Psalm 81:3 is usually used which says:

"Blow on a horn for the Hodesh (New Moon) On Keseh (Full Moon) for the Day of our Hag (Feast)."

According to this "concealed moon theory", the word 'keseh' is from the root aok meaning to cover and therefore means "covered moon" or "concealed moon". Now *according to that interpretation*, the verse which says to blow on a horn on the day of Keseh is really saying "[blow on a horn] on the day of Concealed Moon". However this argument is not supported for the second half of this verse also refers to the day of keseh as "the day of our Feast (Hag)". In scripture the word Hag is associated with the three pilgrimage feasts set up by YHWH back in Exodus. The three Feasts are **Passover, Shavuot** and **Tabernacles.** New Moon day is never called a Hag and cannot possibly be synonymous with Keseh/Hag. It has also been suggested that Keseh refers to Yom Teruah which falls on a New Moon day. However, Yom Teruah is called a moed in the Bible not a Hag, so Keseh/Hag will not work there either.

What does Keseh really mean? It is quite likely that the word Keseh could be related to the word "Kista" from the Aramaic and also the word "Kuseu" from the Assyrian which means "full moon". Hebrew, Aramaic and Assyrian are all *Semitic* languages and often share common roots. This then fits in perfectly with Keseh as the day of the Hag since two of the three pilgrimage Feasts are on the 15th of the month, which is about the time of the full moon. Also, if you continue reading the Psalm, it is talking about the time of leaving Egypt right after the first Passover.

There is another point to consider. There is no actual 'day' of concealed moon. It is a fact that the moon stays concealed anywhere from 1.5 days to a possible 3.5 days in the Middle East. It also was only 1000 years after Moses that the Babylonian astronomers discovered how to **approximately** calculate the conjunction. The Ancient Israelites would have no way of knowing when true conjunction was and therefore would not know what day to observe "Concealed Moon Day". If you are thinking that they could have looked at the waning moon to determine it then remember there is a span of 1.5 to 3.5 days of no moon so what day would they be able to choose?

As to evidence in ancient documents or encyclopedias, I have found none. If someone has such evidence, please let me know. I am always willing to study for truth.

Full Moon

With this next one, there are not many who hold to this, but I want to cover something on it because questions do come up. The thought behind the full moon being New Moon Day is a little tough to explain. Most of what I have heard is that YHWH is a God of light and would therefore start a new month in total light. They claim the sign of the woman in the heavens with the moon at her feet is a full moon. Also, they say the Sun being dark at the time of the death of Yeshua had to be an eclipse and could only happen with a dark moon conjunction which would put a full moon at the beginning of the month. First let us examine the sign in the Heavens. The full sign is that she is 'clothed' in the Sun with the Moon at her feet. This sign is Virgo. She cannot be 'clothed' in the Sun with a full moon at her feet. The moon would be too close for it to be full. As the moon passes the Sun at conjunction, it begins to grow or wax in size. When the Sun is in Virgo with the moon at her feet it is in the fall of the year. The Moon would be only about 2 -3 days from conjunction putting it at first visible crescent, not full. In fact this sign happens every year at Yom Teruah. Now what about the eclipse? We know that an eclipse of the Sun can only happen when the moon is coming into conjunction with it. However, an eclipse has never lasted over a few minutes because the moon is always moving. To have the Sun be dark for *three hours* (Mat 27:45) is not a normal occurrence. It has to be supernatural by the hand of YHWH Himself. Therefore the event was not dependent on natural happenings and could happen anytime of the year. Here are just a couple of the quotes found among the early writings from the 3rd century AD:

AFRICANUS (200-245A.D).

VOL 6.03.03 ANTE-NICENE FATHERS

This darkness Thallus, in the third book of his History, calls, as appears to me without reason, an eclipse of the sun. For the Hebrews celebrate the Passover on the 14th day according to the moon, and the passion of our Saviour fails on the day before the Passover; but an eclipse of the sun takes place only when the moon comes under the sun. And **it cannot happen at any other time but in the interval between the first day of the new moon and the last of the old, that is, at their junction:** how then should an eclipse be supposed to happen when the moon is almost diametrically opposite the sun? Let that opinion pass however; let it carry the majority with it; and let this portent of the world be deemed an eclipse of the sun, like others a portent only to the eye. **Phlegon records that, in the time of Tiberius Caesar, at full moon, there was a full eclipse of the sun from the sixth hour to the ninth - manifestly that one of which we speak**. But what has an eclipse in common with an earthquake, the rending rocks, and the resurrection of the dead, and so great a perturbation throughout the universe? Surely no such event as this is recorded for a long period. But **it was a darkness induced by God**, because the Lord happened then to suffer.

METHODIUS (260-312 A.D.)

Whence, also, they are by a descriptive term called newly-enlightened; 104 the moon ever showing forth anew to them the spiritual **full moon, namely, the period and the memorial of the passion,** until the glory and the perfect light of the great day arise.

In looking for evidence in ancient documents or encyclopedias I also came up blank as to it being called the new moon. Again, if there is such evidence please let me know.

First Visible Crescent

We now come to the final possibility for New Moon Day. It seems amazing to me that the most obvious sign in the heavens showing the new start of something is the first visible crescent of the moon. The natural course of growing out of obscurity and becoming brilliantly full and then declining in size as the month continues until disappearing and preparing to appear to start a new month is a smoothly planned pattern. It is like the Sun's pattern of lightly dawning in the early morning heralding in the day and climbing to the utmost of the sky and then beginning its decent till all that is seen is the glow of final light. If you observe all creation it follows this same path. Everything appears from obscurity, climbing to full growth and then slowly lessening in color, brilliancy, size, strength, or volume. This seems to be the rhythm of life, the rhythm of the Earth, the rhythm of the Heavens. As I stated in the last "Theory", the sign of Virgo is seen every Fall season (at Yom Teruah to be more precise) 2 -3 days after the conjunction of the Sun and Moon, which is when the first sliver of the moon becomes visible to the naked eye. It is hard to ignore the very sign YHWH put there for us to witness every year and then tell us to celebrate a special day of shouting on that very day every year. Some would say that the crescent is a pagan symbol and should not be used. To this I must ask: Who created the moon with all of the various phases through the month? Is it right to give credence to the enemy for corrupting that which was created by YHWH and then given to all nations (Deu 4:19) by calling it pagan?

As for evidence in ancient documents and various dictionaries and encyclopedias, there is much. Again go to "JUST GIVE ME THE FACTS PLEASE".

Just *what* is New Moon Day?   It is not a Sabbath day. It is not one of the "six days" of work. However scripture does mention some restrictions to buying and selling on that day. My opinion is that this verse is referring to Yom Teruah, which was observed like a Sabbath. It is a special day - it has more sacrifices than the Sabbath, so obviously it means something to Father. It is the day that marks the beginning of a new month. *It resets the monthly clock* and establishes the day of the next four Sabbaths. New Moon Day is totally separate from the Sabbath and the six working days. Look at the following verses of scripture and notice that the New Moon day and the Sabbath are always mentioned separately.

*Amo 8:5 Saying: 'When **will the new moon be gone**, that we may sell grain? **and the sabbath**, that we may set forth corn? making the ephah small, and the shekel great, and falsifying the balances of deceit;*

*Num 28:11 And **in the beginnings of your months** ye shall offer a burnt offering unto YHVH; two young bullocks, and one ram, seven lambs of the first year without spot; 12 And three tenth deals of flour for a meat offering, mingled with oil, for one bullock; and two tenth deals of flour for a meat offering, mingled with oil, for one ram; 13 And a several tenth deal of flour mingled with oil for a meat offering unto one lamb; for a burnt offering of a sweet savour, a sacrifice made by fire unto YHVH. 14 And their drink offerings shall be half an hin of wine unto a bullock, and the third part of an hin unto a ram, and a fourth part of an hin unto a lamb: **this is the burnt offering of every month throughout the months of the year**. 15 And one kid of the goats for a sin offering unto YHVH shall be offered, beside the continual burnt offering, and his drink offering.*

*Eze 46:1 Thus saith the Master YHVH; The gate of the inner court that looketh toward the east shall be shut the six working days; but **on the sabbath** it shall be opened, and in the **day of the new moon** it shall be opened.*

*1Ch 23:31 And to offer all burnt sacrifices unto YHVH in **the sabbaths**, in **the new moons**, and on the set feasts, by number, according to the order commanded unto them, continually before YHVH:*

*2Ch 2:4 Behold, I build an house to the name of YHVH my Elohim, to dedicate it to him, and to burn before him sweet incense, and for the continual shewbread, and for the burnt offerings morning and evening, **on the sabbaths**, and **on the new moons**, and on the solemn feasts of YHVH our Elohim. This is an ordinance for ever to Israel.*

*2Ch 31:3 He appointed also the king's portion of his substance for the burnt offerings, to wit, for the morning and evening burnt offerings, and the burnt offerings for **the sabbaths,** and **for the new moons**, and for the set feasts, as it is written in the law of YHVH.*

Let us read a little about restrictions for the Sabbath from a few different sources and compare to New Moon Day.

MISHNA

*Shabbat 6:4 **A man should not go out with a sword, bow, shield, club, or spear. `And if he went out, he is liable to a sin offering**. `R. Eliezer says, "They are ornaments for him." `And sages say, "They are nothing but ugly," `since it is said, "And they shall beat their swords into plowshares and their spears into pruning hooks; nation shall not lift up sword against nation, neither shall they learn war any more Is. 2:4."*

*Exo 16:29 See, for that YHVH hath given you the sabbath, therefore he giveth you on the sixth day the bread of two days; **abide ye every man in his place, let no man go out of his place on the seventh day.***

After reading the above statement from the Mishna

and Exodus, let us read of two incidents in scripture (one of them recorded also in Jasher) reflecting a violation of YHWH's commandment to rest if you use a Gregorian perpetual 7 day Sabbath.

BOOK OF JOSHUA, I KINGS AND EXODUS

*Jos 6:3 And ye shall compass the city, **all the men of war**, going about the city once. Thus shalt thou do six days. 4. And seven priests shall bear seven rams' horns before the ark; **and the seventh day** ye shall compass the city seven times, and the priests shall blow with the horns. 5. And it shall be, that when they make a long blast with the ram's horn, and when ye hear the sound of the horn, all the people shall shout with a great shout; and the wall of the city shall fall down flat, **and the people shall go up every man straight before him.'***

*1Ki 20:26 And it came to pass **at the beginning of the year**, that Bar-hadad gave orders to the Arameans, and went up to Aphek to fight against Israel.*

*1Ki 20:29 And they encamped one over against the other **seven days**. And so it was, **that in the seventh day the battle was joined;** and the children of Israel slew of the Arameans a hundred thousand footmen in one day.*

*Exo 40:1 And YHVH spake unto Moses, saying, 2 **On the first day** of the first month shalt thou **set up the tabernacle** of the tent of the congregation.*

*Exo 40:17 And it came to pass in the first month in the second year, **on the first day of the month, that the tabernacle was reared up**.*

*chapter 88:14 And it was **in the second month, on the first day of the month,** that the Lord said to Joshua, Rise up, behold I have given Jericho into thy hand with all the people thereof; **and all your fighting men** shall go round the city, once each day, thus shall you do for six days. 15 And the priests shall blow upon trumpets, and when you shall hear the sound of the trumpet, all the people shall give a great shouting that the walls of the city shall fall down; all the people shall go up **every man against his opponent.** 16 And Joshua did so according to all that the Lord had commanded him. 17 And **on the seventh day** they went round the city seven times, and the priests blew upon trumpets.*

These two battles and the command from YHWH in Exodus – could not have taken place according to the "rules" of the Sabbath and the statement in the Mishna above if one of the days were the Sabbath. The only way this could have been possible is for the battles to start on a New Moon day, for then the battles would be completed the day before the Sabbath. Look at 1Kings 20:26. This would indicate New Moon day which was the first day of the first month of the New Year. Also, if you look at the first sentence in the Jasher account, you will notice the first day of the month is designated. That would be a New Moon day for that month and the counting of the six working days to the seventh day Sabbath would begin the next day. This would also be the account for 1Kings. With counting New Moon day you would have the Sabbath on the eighth day – the day after the battles ended. The account stated in Exodus as a command from YHWH to Moses says "on the first day of the month". Think of the work it took to do that and prepare Aaron and his sons. Also, why would YHWH break His own command to stay put on the seventh day?

What is New Moon Day? It is not a Sabbath. You can work or war if necessary. It has more sacrifices than the Sabbath, therefore it is considered a day of worship for the gates are open on New Moon Day just like the Sabbath.

My desire is to remember and follow His statutes and ordinances. To hear the call of Elijah and be a repairer of the breach which the enemy has cut out before us and changed our paths.

We have so much to learn about what our Father has set in motion from the beginning. As time draws near for the King's return, YHWH will be revealing more truth to those who seek after it. Don't find yourself waiting for the bus at the wrong corner.

WHY SIGHT THE MOON FROM ISRAEL?

With each new subject the Father reveals to us, the more confusion and opinions can come in, and this subject of when and where to sight the new moon is no different. Should we learn to spot the moon here where we live or should we go with the sighting from the land of Israel? My question to all of us is: Where is home? Do we consider ourselves separate from Judah and therefore not a part of Yah's family? Do we see the land we now live in as the Promised Land? Many of us see who we are in YHWH. We see that we are the wild branch grafted in with the cultured branch and therefore connected to the Tree and Root of our Messiah and YHWH. That means that where the Root is so is the Tree and where the Tree is so are the branches!   Where is the Root?

Lev 25:2 *Speak unto the children of Israel, and say unto them, When ye come into the* **land which I give you**, *then shall the land keep a sabbath unto Yahweh.*

Lev 25:23 *The land shall not be sold forever: for* **the land is mine**; *for ye are strangers and sojourners with me.*

Num 15:2 *Speak unto the children of Israel, and say unto them, When ye be come into the* **land of your habitations, which I give unto you**,

Num 15:18 *Speak unto the children of Israel, and say unto them, When ye come into* **the land whither I bring you,**

Num 20:12 *And Yahweh spake unto Moses and Aaron, Because ye believed me not, to sanctify me in the eyes of the children of Israel, therefore ye shall not bring this congregation into* **the land which I have given them**.

Num 27:12 *And Yahweh said unto Moses, Get thee up into this mount Abarim, and see* **the land which I have given unto the children of Israel.**

Num 34:2 *Command the children of Israel, and say unto them, When ye come into the land of Canaan;* **this is the land that shall fall unto you for an inheritance, even the land of Canaan with the coasts thereof:**

Num 35:34 *Defile not therefore the land which ye shall inhabit,* ***wherein I dwell: for I Yahweh dwell among the children of Israel.***

Deu 4:1 *Now therefore hearken, O Israel, unto the statutes and unto the judgments, which I teach you, for to do them, that ye may live, and go in and possess* ***the land which Yahweh Elohim of your fathers giveth you.***

Deu 31:7 *And Moses called unto Joshua, and said unto him in the sight of all Israel, Be strong and of a good courage: for thou must go with this people unto the* ***land which Yahweh hath sworn unto their fathers to give them; and thou shalt cause them to inherit it.***

Deu 31:23 *And he gave Joshua the son of Nun a charge, and said, Be strong and of a good courage: for thou shalt bring the children of Israel into* ***the land which I sware unto them:*** *and I will be with thee.*

Deu 32:49 *Get thee up into this mountain Abarim, unto mount Nebo, which is in the land of Moab, that is over against Jericho; and* ***behold the land of Canaan, which I give unto the children of Israel for a possession:***

Jos 1:2 *Moses my servant is dead; now therefore arise, go over this Jordan, thou, and all this people, unto* ***the land which I do give to them, even to the children of Israel.***

Isa 2:3 *And many people shall go and say, Come ye, and* ***let us go up to the mountain of Yahweh, to the house of the Elohim of Jacob***; *and he will teach us of his ways, and we will walk in his paths:* ***for out of Zion shall go forth the law, and the word of Yahweh from Jerusalem.***

*Mic 4:1 But in the last days it shall come to pass, that the mountain of the house of Yahweh shall be established in the top of the mountains, and it shall be exalted above the hills; and **people shall flow unto it.** 2 And many nations shall come, and say, Come, and **let us go up to the mountain of Yahweh, and to the house of the Elohim of Jacob;** and he will teach us of his ways, and we will walk in his paths: for **the law shall go forth of Zion, and the word of Yahweh from Jerusalem.***

The Root is in Israel. He has marked this little piece of earth to physically make His stand against the enemy in the last days and place His chosen there. And all His law will come from Him out of His land. In these last days we also must keep our eyes on the picture set by YHWH of the two houses, again being joined together in His hand. Many in Israel are waking up to desire how to sight the moon again. This to me is very exciting. To once again be working hand in hand with brother Judah to repair what the enemy has torn apart, is exactly what Father has proclaimed He will do. I guess I would say to let Judah proclaim New Moon from Zion and let us join them in celebrating it as one family.

*Lev 25:23 The land shall not be sold forever: for **the land is mine**; for ye are strangers and sojourners with me.*

If we agree with this, then where else should we look for the proclamation of the New Moon being seen?

WHEN DOES A DAY BEGIN?

When we discovered that many things we believed were not from YHWH, but were instead traditions of men, some even brought in from pagan practices, we looked for the true path to worship and obey Father. We turned to our brother Judah for direction. This however was not what YHWH wanted. *He* wanted to show us His pure path, for even Judah had strayed from it. They also made their own traditions that kept one from following the pure path of YHWH. They bound tethers around the people, making the obeying of YHWH's commandments burdensome and difficult to understand without a rabbi or priest to interpret. In digging into scripture and history we have been uncovering a simple walk set out by our Father. Deuteronomy 30:11 says:

For this commandment which I command thee this day, it is not too hard for thee, neither is it far off.

This comforting statement is echoed in 1 John 5:3:

For this is the love of Elohim, that we keep his commandments: and his commandments are not grievous.

After the time of the exile the leaders of Judah began putting what we call fences around the Torah of YHWH. This was done by them to protect what He had set down for His people to follow. These fences were referred to by Yeshua as "the traditions of men".

Some of these fences, I am sure, were set with good intensions to keep the people from violating Torah. The big problem was that fence took on the equivalence of a commandment from YHWH Himself.

One fence I am going to expose is when a day really started. Let us again examine Gen. 1:1-5.

Gen 1:1 In the beginning God made the heaven and the earth. 2 But the earth was unsightly and unfurnished, and darkness was over the deep, and the Spirit of God moved over the water. 3 And God said, Let there be light, and there was light. 4 And God saw the light that it was good, and God divided between the light and the darkness. 5 And

71

God called the light Day, and the darkness he called Night, and there was evening and there was morning, the first day.

We all know these verses practically by heart. This, may I suggest, is our problem. It is so familiar to us we don't really see what it is saying. We know that **everything was made by Yeshua and without Him nothing was made**. We know that He is the **Word** made flesh. Therefore, it was by the **word** of Elohim that all was made. Now look at the verses above. What were the **first words** of Elohim? **"Let there be light"**. This was the **beginning of the creating** on the first day. Light was the main object here and had started the first day. The darkness that had covered the earth was now removed from its overbearing position. After this He saw the LIGHT was good, Elohim divided the two. How? The first to be put in place after the calling of light was 'ehreb' (evening – that time when day melts away) and then 'boker' (morning – that time when night retreats from the coming light). This completed the first day and prepared for the next day of creating. Remember, **evening** is not night; it is the *divider* between day and night; and **morning** is not day; it is the *divider* between night and day.

When you hear the statement that the word of YHWH is living, it is so true. How many times have you read a certain book, chapter and verse and said to yourself "wow! I don't remember seeing that before."? Let's explore in His word to see how the beginning of a day was viewed.

Exo 8:20 And **YHVH said unto Moses, Rise up early in the morning, and stand before Pharaoh**; *lo, he cometh forth to the water; and say unto him, Thus says YHVH, Let my people go, that they may serve me. 21 Else, if thou wilt not let my people go, behold, I will send swarms of flies upon thee, and upon thy servants, and upon thy people, and into thy houses: and the houses of the Egyptians shall be full of swarms of flies, and also the ground whereon they are. 22 And I will sever in that day the land of Goshen, in which my people dwell, that no swarms of flies shall be there; to the end thou may know that I am YHVH in the midst of the earth. 23 And I will put a division between my people and thy people:* **tomorrow shall this sign be**.

Exo 9:4 And YHVH shall sever between the cattle of Israel and the cattle of Egypt: and there shall nothing die of all that is the children of Israel. 5 **And YHVH appointed a set time, saying, Tomorrow YHVH shall do this thing in the land**. 6 **And YHVH did that thing on the morrow,** *and all the cattle of Egypt died: but of the cattle of the children of Israel died not one.*

Exo 9:13 **And YHVH said unto Moses, Rise up early in the morning, and stand before Pharaoh,** *and say unto him, Thus says YHVH Elohim of the Hebrews, Let my people go, that they may serve me. 14 For I will at this time send all my plagues upon thine heart, and upon thy servants, and upon thy people; that thou may know that there is none like me in all the earth. 15 For now I will stretch out my hand that I may smite thee and thy people with pestilence; and thou shalt be cut off from the earth. 16 And in very deed for this cause have I raised thee up, for to shew in thee my power; and that my name may be declared throughout all the earth. 17 As yet exalt thou thyself against my people,* *that thou wilt not let them go? 18* **Behold, tomorrow about this time** *I will cause it to rain a very grievous hail, such as hath not been in Egypt since the foundation thereof even until now.*

Exo 10:4 *Else, if thou refuse to let my people go,* **behold, tomorrow will I bring the locusts into thy coast***: 5 And they shall cover the face of the earth, that one cannot be able to see the earth: and they shall eat the residue of that which is escaped, which remains unto you from the hail, and shall eat every tree which grows for you out of the field:*

Exo 10:12 *And YHVH said unto Moses, Stretch out thine hand over the land of Egypt for the locusts, that they may come up upon the land of Egypt, and eat every herb of the land, even all that the hail hath left. 13 And Moses stretched forth his rod over the land of Egypt,* **and YHVH brought an east wind upon the land all that day, and all that night; and when it was morning, the east wind brought the locusts.**

Exo 16:8 *And Moses said, This shall be, when* **YHVH shall give you in the evening flesh** *to eat, and* **in the morning bread** *to the full; for that YHVH hears your murmurings which ye murmur against him: and what are we? Your murmurings are not against us, but against YHVH.*

Exo 16:12 *I have heard the murmurings of the children of Israel: speak unto them, saying,* **At even ye shall eat flesh***, and* **in the morning ye shall be filled with bread***; and ye shall know that I am YHVH your Elohim. 13 And it came to pass, that* **at even the quails came up, and covered the camp***: and* **in the morning the dew lay round about the**

74

host. 14 And when the dew that lay was gone up, behold, upon the face of the wilderness there lay a small round thing, as small as the hoar frost on the ground. 15 And when the children of Israel saw it, they said one to another, it is manna: for they knew not what it was. And Moses said unto them, "This is the bread which YHVH hath given you to eat."

*Exo 16:19 And Moses said, Let no man leave of **it till the morning**. 20 Notwithstanding they hearkened not unto Moses; **but some of them left of it until the morning, and it bred worms, and stank:** and Moses was wroth with them. 21 **And they gathered it every morning,** every man according to his eating: and when the sun waxed hot, it melted.*

*Exo 16:23 And he said unto them, This is that which YHVH hath said, **Tomorrow is the rest of the holy sabbath unto YHVH**: bake that **which ye will bake today**, and seethe that ye will seethe; and that which remains over lay up for you **to be kept until the morning**.*

*Exo 32:5 And when Aaron saw it, he built an altar before it; and Aaron made proclamation, and said, **Tomorrow is a feast to YHVH**. 6 And they **rose up early on the morrow**, and offered burnt offerings, and brought peace offerings; and the people sat down to eat and to drink, and rose up to play.*

*Num 11:32 **And the people stood up all that day, and all that night, and all the next day,** and they gathered the quails: he that gathered least gathered ten homers: and they spread them all abroad for themselves round about the camp.*

Num 14:1 *And all the congregation lifted up their voice, and cried;* **and the people wept that night.** *(14:2-25 - the whole discourse between the people and Joshua, Caleb, Moses and YHVH)*

Num 14:25 *(Now the Amalekites and the Canaanites dwelt in the valley.)* **Tomorrow turn you, and get you into the wilderness by the way of the Red sea.** *(14:26-39 – the judgement of YHVH on the people)*

Num 14:40 *And they* **rose up early in the morning**, *and gat them up into the top of the mountain, saying, Lo, we be here, and will go up unto the place which YHVH hath promised: for we have sinned.*

Num 16:5 *And he spoke unto Korah and unto all his company, saying,* **Even tomorrow YHVH will shew who are his**, *and who is holy; and will cause him to come near unto him: even him whom he hath chosen will he cause to come near unto him. 6 This do; Take you censers, Korah, and all his company; 7 And put fire therein, and put incense in them* **before YHVH tomorrow**: *and it shall be that the man whom YHVH doth choose, he shall be holy: ye take too much upon you, ye sons of Levi.*

1Sa 19:11 *Saul also sent messengers unto David's house, to watch him, and to slay him in the morning: and Michal David's wife told him, saying,* **If thou save not thy life to night, tomorrow thou shalt be slain.**

1Sa 20:5 *And David said unto Jonathan, Behold,* **tomorrow** *is the new moon, and I should not fail to sit with the king at meat: but let me go, that I may hide myself in the field unto the third day at even.*

*2Sa 11:12 **And David said to Uriah, Tarry here today also, and tomorrow I will let thee depart.** So Uriah abode in Jerusalem that day, and the morrow. 13 And when David had called him, he did eat and drink before him; and he made him drunk: **and at even he went out to lie on his bed with the servants of his master,** but went not down to his house. 14 And **it came to pass in the morning**, that David wrote a letter to Joab, and sent it by the hand of Uriah.*

*2Ki 6:28 **And the king said unto her, What ails thee? And she answered, This woman said unto me, Give thy son, that we **may eat him today,** and we will **eat my son tomorrow.** 29 So we boiled my son, and did eat him: and **I said unto her on the next day**, Give thy son, that we may eat him: and she hath hid her son.*

Can anyone see where evening is the beginning of the next day? Just read the 19 verses I have copied from scripture and point that little fact out because I don't see it. There are more places in the Bible that I could have taken time to record here but, really, how many do you need to see to believe? Tomorrow, in the morning, on the morrow was and still is the beginning of the next day.

If we believe that the day begins in the evening, then how do we understand the verses talking about the crucifixion? Reading in Mark 15 we see Yeshua was crucified at the **third hour of the day**. That would be 9 at night, for the first hour of the day would start at 6 in the evening. Then He cried out at the sixth hour (12 midnight) and died at the ninth hour (3 a.m.). Has anybody thought about this?

Now let's look at a couple verses in Mathew, Mark, Luke and John.

Mat 27:57 **Now when evening had come**, *there came a rich man from Arimathea, named Joseph; who himself had also become a disciple of Jesus.58 This man went to Pilate and asked for the body of Jesus. Then Pilate commanded the body to be given to him.59 When Joseph had taken the body, he wrapped it in a clean linen cloth,60 and laid it in his new tomb which he had hewn out of the rock;* **and he rolled a large stone against the door of the tomb, and departed.61 And Mary Magdalene was there, and the other Mary, sitting opposite the tomb. 62 On the next day, which followed the Day of Preparation,** *the chief priests and Pharisees gathered together to Pilate,*

Mar 15:42 **Now when evening had come, because it was the Preparation Day, that is, the day before the Sabbath,**43 *Joseph of Arimathea, a prominent council member, who was himself waiting for the kingdom of God, coming and taking courage, went in to Pilate and asked for the body of Jesus.44 Pilate marveled that He was already dead; and summoning the centurion, he asked him if He had been dead for some time.45 So when he found out from the centurion, he granted the body to Joseph.46 Then he bought fine linen, took Him down, and wrapped Him in the linen.* **And he laid Him in a tomb which had been hewn out of the rock, and rolled a stone against the door of the tomb.47 And Mary Magdalene and Mary the mother of Joses observed where He was laid**

Mar 16:1 **Now when the Sabbath was past,** *Mary Magdalene, Mary the mother of James, and Salome bought* *spices, that they might come and anoint Him.2* **Very early in the morning, on the first day of the week, they came to the tomb when the sun had risen..**

Mar 16:9 **Now when He rose early on the first day of the week**, *He appeared first to Mary Magdalene, out of whom He had cast seven demons.*

Luk 23:44 *Now it was about the sixth hour,* **and there was darkness over all the earth until the ninth hour.***45 Then the sun was darkened and the veil of the temple was torn in two.46 And when Jesus had cried out with a loud voice, He said, "Father, 'into Your hands I commit My spirit.' " Having said this, He breathed His last.*

Luk 23:50 *Now behold, there was a man named Joseph, a council member, a good and just man. 51 He had not consented to their decision and deed. He was from Arimathea, a city of the Jews, who himself was also waiting for the kingdom of God.52* **This man went to Pilate and asked for the body of Jesus.53 Then he took it down, wrapped it in linen**, *and laid it in a tomb that was hewn out of the rock, where no one had ever lain before.54* **That day was the Preparation, and the Sabbath drew near.** *(was dawning-becoming light) 55 And the women who had come with Him from Galilee followed after, and they observed the tomb and how His body was laid.56 Then they returned and prepared spices and fragrant oils.* **And they rested on the Sabbath according to the commandment.**

Luk 24:1 **Now on the first day of the week, very early in the morning**, *they, and certain other women with them, came to the tomb bringing the spices which they had* *prepared.2 But they found the stone rolled away from the tomb.3 Then they went in and did not find the body of the Lord Jesus.*

Joh 19:14 Now it was the Preparation Day of the Passover, and about the sixth hour. *And he said to the Jews, "Behold your King!"*

Joh 19:31 Therefore, because it was the Preparation Day, that the bodies should not remain on the cross on the Sabbath *(for that Sabbath was a high day), the Jews asked Pilate that their legs might be broken, and that they might be taken away.*

Joh 19:38 *After this, Joseph of Arimathea, being a disciple of Jesus, but secretly, for fear of the Jews, asked Pilate that he might take away the body of Jesus; and Pilate gave him permission.* **So he came and took the body of Jesus.***39 And Nicodemus, who at first came to Jesus by night, also came, bringing a mixture of myrrh and aloes, about a hundred pounds.40 Then they took the body of Jesus, and bound it in strips of linen with the spices, as the custom of the Jews is to bury.41 Now in the place where He was crucified there was a garden, and in the garden a new tomb in which no one had yet been laid.42 **So there they laid Jesus, because of the Jews' Preparation Day, for the tomb was nearby.***

Joh 20:1 Now on the first day of the week Mary Magdalene went to the tomb early, *while it was still dark, and saw that the stone had been taken away from the tomb.*

Joh 20:19 Then, the same day at evening, being the first day of the week, *when the doors were shut where the* *disciples were assembled, for fear of the Jews, Jesus came and stood in the midst, and said to them, "Peace be with you."*

Do you see anywhere in these verses it says the day starts at evening? Read the bolded parts carefully. Evening is always the latter part of that day. Also, remember, the preparation day was the day before Sabbath and if Sabbath is the 7th day which is the LAST day of the week, then the women came the very next day after Sabbath; which was the FIRST day of the new week.   I would like to pause here and examine a verse in Mathew.

Mat 28:1 In the end G3796 of the sabbath,G4521 as it began to dawnG2020 towardG1519 the firstG3391 day of the week,G4521 cameG2064 MaryG3137 MagdaleneG3094...

Let us examine each word as best as we can. First, you will notice that the word 'Sabbath' and 'week' have the same Greek word number. It has the look that there are two Sabbaths in a row here. However, let us dig deeper into the Hebraic meaning of these two. The word '**end**' which is the first description of the 'Sabbath' means - *late in the day; by extension after the close of the day. to the back, that is, aback (as adverb or preposition of time or place; or as noun): - after, back (-ward), (+ get) behind, + follow.*

The second word '**dawn**' following the word 'Sabbath' means - *to begin to grow light: - begin to dawn. to illuminate (figuratively): - give light. to shine upon, that* *is, become (literally) visible or (figuratively) known: - appear, give light.*

So, reading the first part of this verse it is saying – late in the day, after the close of the Sabbath, as it began to grow light, to illuminate.

Let's refresh our understanding of what this time of the year was for the Hebrews: This was the Passover time which consisted of the Passover meal the evening of the 14th of Abib, The day of Unleavened Bread the 15th of Abib and the day of First Fruits (waving of the omer at the temple) on the 16th, which began the counting of the 7 perfect (undefiled) weeks to Shavuot (Feast of **Weeks**). Lev. 23:15

Ok, let us continue.

"toward the first" – meaning – *to the one or first.* Remember the instructions in Leviticus: "count 7 Sabbaths perfect (or undefiled)." So this phrase *'toward the first'* is pointing to the beginning day (first) of the count of the perfect Sabbath week; 6 days work, 7th rest.

The Greek word – 'sabbaton' is the same as the Hebrew word for Sabbath. It is not a plural word. So, the verse of Mathew 28:1 really reads like this: *Late in the day, after the close of the Sabbath, as it began to grow light and illuminate toward the first of the 7 perfect weeks count.*

By understanding what this sentence says, you can actually see the day ending on the dawn of a new sunrise. I hope this is helpful for clarifying the double use of the Greek word 'sabbaton'.

I Thes 5:5 You are all sons of light and sons of day. We are not of the night nor of darkness.

There are several quotes from different sources which are also found in the "JUST GIVE ME THE FACTS PLEASE" collection.

Just because we have shown the error of thinking the day (especially Sabbath) starts in the evening does not mean the wonderful dinner that marks the end of a busy week and heralds in the Sabbath the next morning should be stopped. What this information does uncover is that we are not violating any commandment if we finish up chores that evening before tucking ourselves in bed and waking to a beautiful day of resting.

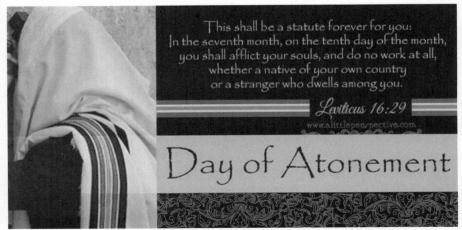

This shall be a statute forever for you:
In the seventh month, on the tenth day of the month,
you shall afflict your souls, and do no work at all,
whether a native of your own country
or a stranger who dwells among you.

Leviticus 16:29
www.alittleperspective.com

Day of Atonement

WHAT DO WE DO ABOUT DAY OF ATONEMENT?

This is a question that many say "throws a wrench" in the works for a lunar based Sabbath. Does it really? Let us look at the verses in Leviticus and examine them.

*Lev 16:29 And this shall be a statute forever unto you: that in the seventh month, on the tenth day of the month, ye shall afflict your souls, and do no work at all, whether it be one of your own country, or a stranger that sojourneth among you:30 For on that day shall the priest make an atonement for you, to cleanse you, that ye may be clean from all your sins before YHVH.31 **It shall be a sabbath of rest** unto you, and **ye shall afflict your souls**, by a statute forever.*

*Lev 16:34 And this shall be an everlasting statute unto you, **to make an atonement for the children of Israel for all their sins once a year.** And he did as YHVH commanded Moses.*

Lev 23:27 Also **on the tenth day** *of this seventh month there shall be a day of atonement: it shall be an holy convocation unto you; and* **ye shall afflict your souls**, *and offer an offering made by fire unto YHVH.28 And ye shall do no work in that same day: for it is a day of atonement,* **to make an atonement for you before YHVH your Elohim.**29 *For whatsoever soul it be that shall not be afflicted in that same day, he shall be cut off from among his people.30 And whatsoever soul it be that doeth any work in that same day, the same soul will I destroy from among his people.31 Ye shall do no manner of work: it shall be a statute for ever throughout your generations in all your dwellings.32 It shall be unto you* **a sabbath of rest**, *and ye shall afflict your souls:* **in the ninth day of the month at even, from even unto even,** *shall ye celebrate* **your sabbath**. *(shabbathchem)*

After reading the above scriptures; let's look at a few things. First of all, this is the only time in YHWH's instructions to His appointed times that He tells us to begin on *the evening of the day before* the 10th (Lev 23:32). Next, this is not THE Sabbath. It is A sabbath of rest – in Hebrew that is Shabbat shabbathon. If you look at the instructions for Yom Teruah right before this, you will see this is also a shabbathon with no work. If you look at the tenth as THE Sabbath, then you must look at the first day of the month also that way and if you do that you now have 9 days to the next Sabbath. These two times are not THE Sabbath. Both of these times were set up by YHWH for a special purpose. They are a shadow of something to come just like all His appointed times. So, what is Day of Atonement a shadow of? Many of us have seen the fulfillment of this day through Yeshua and his death on the cross. Let us examine that event closer.

On the evening of the 13th (according to John) after Yeshua and His disciples had their Passover together, they went to the Mount of Olives and there in the garden our Master began His afflicting of soul. His "afflicting" continued through the night into the morning and didn't stop until He gave up his spirit. It **went from evening until evening;** just as it was commanded in Leviticus. Yeshua became the ram of the sin offering and went through the fire for us to cleanse us of sin. This was done only once a year, why? Because He did it ONCE for all (Lev.16:34). Forever is this atonement placed before YHWH in His Temple. On this do we meditate each year this kadosh day comes. There is one other item to remember; we do not fast on the weekly Sabbath.

SUN-WORSHIP AND THE ORIGIN OF SUNDAY

Chapter 6   Samuele Bacchiocchi, Ph. D., Andrews University

"How would fasting on the Sabbath demonstrate hatred against the "evil" God of the Jews? The answer is to be found in the fact that for the Jews the Sabbath was anything but a day of fast or of mourning. **Even the strictest Jewish sects objected to fasting on the Sabbath. The rabbis, though they differed in their views regarding the time and number of the Sabbath meals, agreed that food on the Sabbath ought to be abundant and good. The following statement epitomizes perhaps the typical rabbinic view: "Do you think that I (God) gave you the Sabbath as burden? I gave it to you for your benefit.' How? Explained** *Rabbi Hiyya bar Abba(180-230 ad),* **'Keep the**

Sabbath holy with food, drink and clean garment, enjoy yourself and I shall reward you."

FELLOW BELIEVERS:

Christmas **is** the Winter Solstice
Easter **is** Ostara (the Spring Equinox)
Halloween **is** Samhain
Valentine's Day **is** Imbolc
May Day **is** Beltane
Sunday **is** the sun's day
Monday **is** the moon's day
Tuesday **is** Tyr's (Tiw's) Day
Wednesday **is** Woden's (Odin's) Day
Thursday **is** Thor's Day
Friday **is** Freya's Day
Saturday **is** Saturn's Day

THIS CALENDAR IS PAGAN!

Okay, so here are my questions...

Where did the Catholic Church get the authority to change the day of rest to Sunday? Is it in scripture? Where did they get the authority to make December 25th the birthday of the Messiah? Or change Passover to Easter?

Where did the Jewish Rabbis get the authority to change the calendar from what YHWH set up at the beginning to what is followed now? Who gave them authority to set in place rules of postponement, start the day at night or line up the Sabbath with the Roman calendar? *Is it in scripture?*

And finally, If YHWH has said to bring no other gods before His face, and we know that celebrating Christmas, Easter and calling Sunday His day is doing just that; why, then, do we insist He lined up His Sabbath with the pagan day of Saturn on a pagan, Roman calendar? Wasn't it created by Julius Caesar around 45 BC; and fashioned after the solar calendar of the Egyptians whose main god was the sun god Ra? And weren't the months and days named after and honored to their pagan gods? Doesn't that go against His very nature of holiness and seem a bit compromising to His command?

YHWH set things in order for man to follow in the very beginning. He set the sun in place to show the length of a full year. It also displayed the length of the day by rising and setting *(Gen.1:5 - And Elohim called the light 'day' and the darkness He called 'night.' And there came to be evening and there came to be morning,).* He set the moon in place to account for the months by counting out the days from the new crescent to the reappearing of the next by its waxing and waning. Within that month of days, YHWH set up His appointed times throughout the year.....including His Sabbath. YHWH is not an Elohim of confusion. He did not give instructions for postponements so feasts and fasts don't collide.

Is it possible that after we learned about the deception of the wrong rest day and holidays that maybe....*just maybe* we need to really look at the calendar with more openness? When following the heavenly calendar, we are **not** changing any calendar...we are **leaving** the "Babylonian" one (coming out of Egypt) and **returning to** YHWH's with His instructions of keeping the appointed times **by His time table.**

I will end with this:

To the doubter NO amount of evidence is sufficient enough.

JUST GIVE ME THE FACTS PLEASE!

Before you begin to read the following information, please put on your "thinking cap" and **study** the statements made by each source.   I think one of the most common things to do is look for any discrepancy between statements so the whole subject can be thrown to the wind as unreliable; however, if you would be more objective in your examination and realize that **they all agree it was this way** – they just don't agree or understand **how it was carried out** for too much time has elapsed for us. It is like digging up old bones and not arguing their existence, but trying to agree **how** they got there. Keep this in mind........skimming only gives you fuel for argument....READING gives you understanding.

My few comments in this chapter are prefaced by the word '**NOTE**'.

JEWISH ENCYCLOPEDIA

WEEK   (Connection with Lunar Phases)
*A division of time comprising seven days, thus explaining the Hebrew name. There are indications of the use of another system of reckoning time, in which the month was divided into three parts of ten days each, the decade being designated in Hebrew by the term " 'asor" (Gen. xxiv. 55; comp. the commentaries of Dillmann and Holzinger ad loc.; Ex. xii. 3; Lev. xvi. 29, xxiii. 27, xxv. 9). This apparently represented one-third of the solar month, **while the week of seven days was connected with the lunar month, of which***

*it is, approximately, a fourth. **The quadripartite division of the month was evidently in use among the Hebrews and other ancient peoples;** but it is not clear whether it originated among the former. It is unnecessary to assume, however, that it was derived from the Babylonians, for it is equally possible that observations of the four phases of the moon led the Hebrew nomads spontaneously and independently to devise the system of **dividing the interval between the successive new moons into four groups of seven days each.** There is ground, on the other hand, for the assumption that both among the Babylonians and among the Hebrews the first day of the first week of the month was always reckoned as coincident with the first day of the month. **The emphasis laid on the requirement (Lev. xxiii. 15) that the weeks of Pentecost should be "complete" (temimot) suggests that weeks might be reckoned in such a way as to violate this injunction.** This was the case as long as the first day of the first week of the month was made to coincide with the new moon. At the end of four weeks an interval of one or two days might intervene before the new week could begin. **At an early date, however, this intimate connection between the week and the moon must have been dissolved,** the chief cause of the fixed week of seven days being, in all probability, the predominance of the seventh day as the Sabbath... The week thus became a useful standard in the measurement of intervals of time (one week, Gen. xxix. 27 et seq.; two weeks, Lev. xii. 5; three weeks, Dan. x. 2; seven weeks, Deut. xvi. 9; Lev. xxiii. 15).*

CALENDAR   (lunar origin)

*The Sabbath depending, in Israel's nomadic period, upon the observation of the phases of the moon, **it could not, according to this view, be a fixed day**. When the Israelites* *settled in the land and became farmers, their new life would have made it desirable that the Sabbath should come at regular intervals and the desired change would have been made easily as they had abandoned the lunar religion. The moon was the beneficent deity of the shepherds in the region and climate where ancient Israel had its ancestral home. Hence the many traces of lunar institutions in even the latest Israelitish cult and its phraseology; e.g., the "horn" (crescent), the "face" (of YHWH) in the benedictions, etc.* **The Sabbath, as marking the end of the week, reveals its lunar origin**; *the phases of the moon having taught the shepherds, whose weal or wo depended so largely upon the benevolence or malevolence of the night season, to divide the period elapsing between two new moons into four equal groups (weeks), the last day of each—in imitation of the moon's coming to rest, as it were—becoming the day of rest.* **Indications are not wanting that at first the New Moon festival was not counted among the seven days of the week; but after 7 X 4 (=28) days had elapsed, one or two days were intercalated as New Moon days, whereupon a new cycle of four weeks began, so that the Sabbath was a movable festival.** *Later the week and the Sabbath became fixed; and this gradually resulted in taking away from the New Moon festival its popular importance.*

UNIVERSAL JEWISH ENCYCLOPEDIA, (1943)

HOLIDAYS p.410

"1. Sabbath and New Moon (Rosh Hodesh), both periodically recurring in the course of the year. **The New Moon is still, and the Sabbath originally was, dependent upon the lunar cycle.** Both date back to the nomadic period of Israel. Originally the New Moon was celebrated in the same way as the Sabbath; gradually it became less important, while the Sabbath became more and more a day of religion and humanity, of religious meditation and instruction, or peace and delight of the soul, and produced powerful and beneficent effects outside of Judaism."

WEEK p.482

Shabbat [weekly Sabbath] **originally arose from the lunar cycle**, containing four weeks ending in Sabbath, plus one or two additional unreckoned days per [lunar] month." "With the development of the importance of the Sabbath as a day of consecration and the emphasis laid upon the significant number seven, **the week became more and more divorced from its lunar connection".**

NEW MOON p.171

"However, in the diaspora, the New Moon came to occupy a secondary position, in contrast to **"a so called Saturday sabbath"**; the prohibition against work and the carrying on of commerce was lifted, and the New Moon, although still celebrated by means of increased offerings, soon was reduced to the rank of a minor of half- holiday. **The importance of [sighting] a new moon [crescent] was confined to the fact that it remained of great value and necessity for the fixing of the festivals."**

HISTORY OF THE TALMUD

APPENDIX B

But as our present reformers are descendants of the Pharisees, and the Sadducees being no more in existence, therefore they also have in many things adopted a new form, and recognize the teachings of the Pharisees (as for instance the observance of the sixth day of Sivan as Pentecost) as indisputable laws. But we can by no means accuse the reformers in not believing in tradition generally, as we cannot well accuse of that the former Sadducees. *(Even those reformers who have changed the Sabbath, for even this can be explained in accordance with the general rule of the Talmud which sanctifies the seventh day, but not the Sabbath itself, and for this reason the Talmud decreed that in case one forgets which day is the Sabbath, he shall count six days and observe the seventh as Sabbath, see our article in the Deborah, 1894.)*

NOTE: Can I just ask a question here? If the Jews had always observed the Sabbath on Saturday, how could they forget which day it was?

ENCYCLOPAEDIA OF RELIGION AND ETHICS (1908)

JEWISH CALENDAR   p.117

*"The Assuan Papyri yield ample proof of the fact that at the time after the exile, **no such fixed [week] cycle was in use among the Jews,** and this would appear to be true also of the Talmudic period."*

THE POPULAR AND CRITICAL BIBLE ENCYCLOPEDIA, (1904)

"It is powerfully urged by the believers in a primitive Sabbath, that we find from time immemorial the knowledge of a week of 7 days among all nations-- Egyptians, Arabians, Indians -- in a word, all the nations of the East, have in all ages **made use of this week of 7 days, for which it is difficult to account without admitting that this knowledge was derived from the common ancestors [Adam and Eve] of the human race. Among all early nations the lunar months were the readiest large divisions of time...(and was divided in 4 weeks), corresponding (to) the phases or the quarters of the moon.** In order to connect the reckoning by weeks with the lunar month, we find that all ancient nations observed some peculiar solemnities to mark the day of the New Moon."

THE NEW SCHAFF-HERZOG ENCYCLOPEDIA OF RELIGIOUS KNOWLEDGE

VOL.10 p.135

"The association of sabbath rest with the account of creation must have been very ancient among the Hebrews, and it is noteworthy that no other Semitic peoples, even the Babylonians, have any tradition of the creation in six days. **It would appear that the primitive Semites had four chief moondays, probably the first, eighth, fifteenth, and twenty-second of each month, called sabbaths from the fact that there was a tendency to end work before them so that they might be celebrated joyfully.**"

ENCYCLOPEDIA BIBLICA

WEEK   VOL IV   p.705

This quadripartite **division of the month into weeks** was naturally suggested by the phases of the moon and **was far from being peculiar to the Hebrews**.

....**by dividing the first 28 days of each month into four weeks** terminating respectively on the 7th, 14th, 21st, 28th days, and by making the first week of the new moon always begin with the new moon. **This intimate connection however, between the week and the month was soon dissolved.**

SABBATH   VOL IV   p.4178

Astrology is in its nature an occult science, and there is not the slightest trace of a day of twenty-four hours among the ancient Hebrews, who had the week and the Sabbath long before they had any acquaintance with the planetary science of the Babylonian priests......These facts make it safe to reject one often-repeated explanation of the Sabbath viz., that it was in its origin what it is in the astrological week, the day sacred to Saturn,....
...in fact, the four quarters of the moon supply an obvious division of the month.....
"of celebrating a sabbath every 7th day, irrespective of the relationship of the day to the moon's phases, **led to a complete separation from the ancient view of the Sabbath".**

STARS   VOL IV   p.432

The Hebrew month is a lunar month, and the quarter of this period – **one phase of the moon – appears to have determined the week of seven days.**

ENCYCLOPEDIA BRITANICA

We note (a) that in the worship of Yahweh the sacred seasons of **new moon and Sabbath are obviously lunar.**

SCRIBNER'S DICTIONARY OF THE BIBLE
1989 p.521

"In the time of the earliest prophets, **the New Moon stood in the same line with another lunar observance, the Sabbath.**

SABBATH -1909 edit.   p.807
In the prophetic and historical books 'Sabbath' and 'New Moon' are associated in such a way as **to suggest that both were lunar festivals.** *(Am 8:5, Ho 2:11, Is 1:13, 2King 4:23)*

TIME - 1909 edit.   p.36
The next obvious division of time would be the month. **The phases of the moon would be watched, and it would soon be noticed that these recurred at regular intervals...** *Given this period of 28 days, together with the recurrent phases of the moon, it would naturally be subdivided, like the day itself,* **into four divisions or weeks of seven days each.**

HILLEL II

Patriarch (330-365A.D.); son and successor of Judah III. Tradition ascribes to him an enactment which proved of incalculable benefit to his coreligionists of his own and of subsequent generations. **To equalize the lunar with the** *solar year, and thereby render possible the universal celebration of the festivals on the days designated in the Bible, occasional intercalations of a day in a month and of a month in a year were required.*

During the persecutions under Hadrian and in the time of his successor, Antoninus Pius, the martyr Rabbi Akiba and his pupils attempted to lay down rules for the intercalation of a month.

Under the patriarchate of Simon III (140-163) a great quarrel arose concerning the feast-days and the leap-year, which threatened to cause a permanent schism between the Babylonian and the Palestinian communities—a result which was only averted by the exercise of much diplomacy.

In 325 the Council of Nice was held, and by that time the equinox had retrograded to March 21. This council made no practical change in the existing civil calendar, but **addressed itself to the reform of the Church calendar, which was soli-lunar on the Jewish system**. Great disputes had arisen as to the time of celebrating Easter. Moreover, the Church was not fully established, many Christians being still simply Jewish sectarians. A new rule was therefore made, which, while still keeping Easter dependent on the moon, prevented it from coinciding with Passover.

The persecutions under Constantius finally decided the patriarch, Hillel II (330-365), to publish rules for the computation of the calendar, which had hitherto been regarded as a secret science.

The weeks do not continue in a regular cycle regardless of the moon. Each month has four weeks, the beginning with the New Moon. I have no doubt that this was the old Hebrew system.

REST DAYS BY HUTTON WEBSTER

In the year 1869 the late George Smith, well known as a pioneer student of Assyriology, discovered among the cuneiform tablets in the British Museum "a curious religious calendar of the Assyrians, **in which every month is divided into four weeks, and the seventh days, or 'Sabbaths,' are marked out as days on which no work should be undertaken."** ^ Six years afterward Sir Henry Rawlinson published this calendar in the fourth volume of his standard collection of cuneiform inscriptions. It appears to be a transcript of a much more ancient Babylonian original, possibly belonging to the age of Hammurabi (1792-1750 BC), which had been made by order of Asshurbanipal and placed in his royal library at Nineveh.

It has been held, in the first place, that the "evil days" were selected as corresponding to the moon's successive changes; **hence that the seventh day marks the close of the earliest form of the seven-day week, a week bound up with the lunar phases.** According to another opinion the setting apart of every seventh day was due to the importance ascribed to seven; **hence that the seven-day cycles were not regarded as quarters of the lunation but rather as periods containing the symbolic number of seven days, which** *happened to coincide, roughly, with a fourth part of the lunar month.* The second view would be merely an amplification of the first, if we assume, with perhaps the majority of Assyriologists, that **the role of seven as a symbolic number is ultimately connected with the moon changing her phases at intervals of approximately seven days.**

LUNAR CALENDARS AND THE WEEK
The early Christians had at first adopted the Jewish seven-day week with its numbered weekdays,^ but **by the close of the third century a.d. this began to give way to the planetary week ; and in the fourth and fifth centuries the pagan designations became generally accepted in the western half of Christendom.** *During these same centuries the spread of Oriental solar worships,* **especially that of Mithra,^ in the Roman world, had already led to the substitution by pagans of dies Soils for dies Saturni, as the first day of the planetary week ; and Constantine's famous edict, as we have seen, definitely enrolled Sunday among the holidays of the Roman state religion.^**

THE HEBREW SABBATH
But the problem is simplified if we hold that the Hebrews employed lunar seven-day weeks, *perhaps for several centuries preceding the Exile;* **weeks, that is**, *which ended with special observances on the seventh day but none the less were* **tied to the moon's course.**

The establishment of a periodic week ending in a Sabbath observed every seventh day was doubtless responsible for the gradual obsolescence of the new moon festival *as a period of general abstinence,* **since with continuous weeks the new-moon day and the Sabbath Day would from time to time coincide.**

SHAWUI SABBATH: ANCIENT SABBATH OBSERVANCE

"Most theologians and some scholars assume that mainstream Jewish society, at the time of Jesus...was practicing a fixed seven-day week which was the same as the modern fixed [cycling planetary designations] seven-day week. This is extremely doubtful. **The change, from a lunar to a fixed week, was brought about by the power and influence of Rome.** As long as the Nazarenes held power in Jerusalem, all Roman practices and customs, including that of the consecutive week, were held at bay."

"Early historical records clearly confirm that **very early Gentile Christians also kept the same Sabbath as the Nazarenes.** This practice was first changed by "[Pope] Sixtus in 126 AD, and later officially changed by a royal Roman decree from the emperor Constantine. Observance of the Sabbath day was made illegal and observance of a "Sunday" of a fixed [cycling planetary designated] week was made mandatory for all except farmers. **Previous to this time the Roman Saturday was the first day of the Roman week.** The veneration of the Sun **in the second century AD** began to pressure Roman culture to change the first day of their week from Saturn Day to Sunday."

MISHNA

Rosh Hashshana 1:4 On the occasion of two new moons [witnesses to the new moon] violate [the prohibitions of] the Sabbath: `at Nisan and at Tishre. `For on these occasions the messengers go forth to Syria. `And on them they determine the set feasts. `**And when the Temple stood, they violate [the prohibitions of] the**

103

Sabbath on the occasion of all of the [months], `because of the determination of the offering [for the celebration of the new month].

BABYLONIAN TALMUD   02-ROSH-03

Mishnas IV. To VII. For the sake of (the new moon), of the two months Nissan and Tishri, witnesses may profane the Sabbath. **Formerly they profaned the Sabbath for all (new moons),** *but* **since the destruction of the Temple** *they instituted that* **(witnesses) might profane the Sabbath only on account of Nissan and Tishri.** *It once happened that more than forty pair (of witnesses) were on the highway (to Jerusalem) on the Sabbath. Shagbar, the superintendent of Gader, detained them, and (when) R. Gamaliel (heard of it, he) sent and dismissed him. It once happened, that Tobias the physician, his son, and his freed slave saw the new moon in Jerusalem. The explanation of the passage Exodus xii. 1, by R. Simeon and the rabbis. Who are incompetent witnesses? Gamblers with dice, etc.,*

NOTE: How could the Sabbath be in danger of being profaned *every* month? Only on a lunar calendar could this happen; for the last Sabbath of every month is the 29th day and then they would watch the evening sky for the new crescent. The witnesses would then head out for Jerusalem to report.

NOTE: The next reference is from the Zohar. The Zohar is a mystical commentary on the Torah. What is being discussed is the connection of the heavenly realm and the earthly realm pertaining to time according to the two lights created. Notice it is not a contention of whether the moon is for determining the days – only whether the heavenly elements are under it too.

THE ZOHAR

CHAPTER XXIII p.201

but through the serpent they became separated; hence it is written, 'Let them be for lights in the firmament of the Heaven,' to give light upon the earth, instead of 'Let them enlighten the earth,' and therefore we conclude that **both in heaven above and on earth below, time is measured by the courses of the moon."**

Said Rabbi Simeon: **"By the moon's courses, the solstices and days are reckoned and determined."**

Rabbi Eleazar objected to this statement and said: "Is not frequent mention made of fractions of time in the world on high?"

Said Rabbi Simeon in reply: **"Only in the angelic world is there no need of the lunar courses as elements for calculating time,** and when any mention is made of them it is by way of accommodation **to the understanding of the dwellers on earth**."

Again Rabbi Eleazar made objection and said: "It is however written, 'Let them be for signs and seasons, 'Gen. 1:14 that is, for the measurement of time, and these words being in the plural, we may infer that they apply to both worlds having the same unit of measure."

Said Rabbi Simeon in reply: **"The word othoth (signs) is written defectively to show that divisions of time exist not in the world above as in the world below."**

Said Rabbi Eleazar: "Why then is it written, 'Let them be for signs and for seasons,' and from which we may gather that the sun and moon together were to be used for this purpose that the moon is only needed?" Said Rabbi Simeon: "The moon is designated by a plural term, as it resembles a casket filled with various jewels that is oft time spoken of in the plural. Observe that every numerical calculation begins with unity, whatever its value and worth may be or whatever it represents. Now the **Divine Unit** is that in which **everything is included** and **therefore beyond and above all mathematical calculation.** It is the basic unit from which all things in the world take their origin and beginning, and **its analogy in the phenomenal material world is the moon, which is the base of all calculations in connection with the solstices, feasts, SABBATHS;** and **therefore it is that Israel, who belongs to the Holy One, begins the division of time from the various phases and aspects of the moon, symbol of the divine point or unit;** and therefore it is written, 'Ye are attached or joined unto the Lord your God' (Deuter 4-4).

CLEMENT   THE STROMATA

BOOK VI, CHAPTER 16

"In periods of seven days, the moon undergoes its changes. **At the end of the first week**, she becomes half moon; **at the end of the second** [week], full moon; and **at the end of the third** [week], in her wane, again half moon; and **at the end of the fourth** [week] she disappears".

EMIL SCHURER - "THE JEWISH PEOPLE IN THE TIME OF JESUS CHRIST,"

p.366

*"But unless all indications are deceitful, they (Jews) **did not** in the time of [Yahshua Messiah] **possess as yet any fixed calendar**, but on the basis of purely empirical observation, on each occasion they begin a new month with the appearing of the new moon,*

THEODORE GILMAN (1916)

p. 479

*"The changes in the calendric position of the weekly religious rest day have been few from pre-historic times to the present day. **The Sabbath** which came down to the Jews from pre-historic [prior to Moses] times **was the seventh day of the lunar week**. The lunar week and the lunar month gave the simplest form of time division to early man . . . Moon and month meant the same thing. The division of the month into four weeks of seven days left the so-called epagomenal days which had to be neglected, and **the weekly division begun again at the time of the next new moon. The change from the lunar week to the seven-day week running continuously through the year, while a momentous change, was unrecorded.** The use of two styles of weeks seems to have existed together, and the more modern seven-day week slowly, but finally, supplanted its ancient but inexact competitor. The lunar week was simple and serviceable . . . . . . **When the continuous seven-day week was generally accepted, then it was linked with the past, as we now date events before Christ by a scale***

unknown to the people and historians of those times. . .
The lunar Sabbath was succeeded by the seven-day weekly
Sabbath without confusion, and the mention of the
Sabbath in Exodus 31:13 and elsewhere may be taken to
refer to the lunar day." Sunday the World's Rest Day, "The
Sabbath, the Day Which Divine Love Established and
Human Love Must Preserve," Published for the New York
Sabbath Committee, Doubleday, Page and Company, New
York

DR. JULIAN OBERMANN

Jewish Professor of Semitic Languages at Yale University

"The plain fact is that, as seen by recent scholars, **the
system of the fixed calendar was not developed until fully
three to four centuries after** the close of the talmudic
period, about A.D. 485.
Nor can anything be found in the Talmud about such
weighty calendric matters as ...the 'four postponements,'
...the 19-year cycle, ... Above all, there is nothing known in
the old sources about ...starting points of calendric
computations."

[Encyclopedia] Judaica adds: "Also the four dehiyyot
[rules of postponement] developed gradually," noting that
the general acceptance of one of the four rules "**is not
earlier than the tenth century....**"

JEWISH THEOLOGICAL SEMINARY OF AMERICA

Letter by Louis Finkelstein to Dr. L. E. Froom, Feb. 20, 1939.

"The present Jewish calendar was fixed [continuous weekly cycle] **in the fourth century.***"*

JAMES DWYER
"Advanced Astronomy In Bible Texts", & "A New Look At The Christian Sabbath"

"The Early Christian descriptions of a weekly cycle containing periodic single days are very clear, and this information (coupled with evidence provided by the measurable lunar/solar phenomena) **strongly indicates that early Christians were practicing a lunar-based calendar".**

"It now seems almost certain that some additional definitions of the early Sabbath cycle are missing from the modern tradition of the seven-day week. **Essentially, the modern week, as a continuous cycle** *of seven days,* **does not seem to equate to the definition of the week as it was used during the Early Christian era."**

"This new research looks at the Sabbath calendar, as it would have been known to a mainstream Jew, **living in the second temple era, and it finds the Sabbath to have been a rather sophisticated interface with the lunar-solar system.** *In this earlier time,* **the Sabbath cycle,** *surprisingly,* **was defined by the phases of the moon,** *and, even more surprising than this, the* **Sabbath cycle also revolved into precise alignment with the Annual Feast Circuit".**

HERSCHEL SHANKS
Biblical Archaeology Society

"There were very marked differences, in the attitude toward government and the preservation of Jewish

religion and life, between the Palestinian and Babylonian Jews. The Palestinian Jews jealously guarded their religion and way of life, while the Babylonian Jews were clearly, willing to accommodate the government of their area and compromise certain principles they held. This included the Sabbath day. During this time, a major revival of the Zoroastrian religion, took place in (226 A.D.), when the first Sassanian king, Ardeshir, came to the Persian throne. He made reforms to the old lunar-based calendar, which had a far-reaching effect on his people, (especially the Jews), who initially rejected his new calendar, since it affected their religious observances. This resulted, for a while, in two calendars, one decreed by the king and the other, older one, followed by the majority of the people in the kingdom. Eventually, however, the new calendar won out and the Persians, as well as the Jews of Babylonia, began to organize their Sabbaths, according to the new solar calendar."

PATRICK MADRID
Roman Catholic scholar and apologist, 2006,

What your brother-in-law may not understand is that the Catholic Church did not change that commandment. The Catholic Church observes the commandment to keep holy the Lo- . . . the Sabbath, but it does so on the Lord's Day, and the earliest Christians transferred their observance of that commandment from Saturday to Sunday.

First of all, because there was a distinct break between the Old Testament requirements and they wanted to show that Christianity was distinct from Judaism. It came from Judaism, but it was distinct from it. Uh, celebrating the Lord's coming, I'm sorry, celebrating the Lord's resurrection and death on the day that He rose from the dead seemed to be the most appropriate.

Uh, the other thing that we should remember, too, is that **our calendar that we follow, including Seventh-day Adventists, is not only a calendar that was devised by the Catholic Church, but also it is a calendar that's based upon the solar year, not the lunar year. And the Jewish calendar that was observed in the time of Christ is, follows a lunar calendar, which is several days short of the solar calendar.** So the great irony is that even the Seventh-day Adventists themselves **are not worshiping on exactly the same Sabbath day as the Jews of the time of Christ, because it's several days off now, uh, having, uh, switched to [from?] following the lunar calendar.**

EVIATOR ZERUBAVEL, THE SEVEN DAY CIRCLE:

THE HISTORY AND MEANING OF THE WEEK
The Free Press, New York, 1985, p. 11.

Quasi [lunar] weeks and [continuous] weeks actually represent two fundamentally distinct modes of temporal organization of human life, the former involving partial adaptation to nature, and **the latter stressing total emancipation** from it. **The invention of the continuous week** was therefore one of the most significant breakthroughs in human beings' attempts to break away from being prisoners of nature **[and from under God's law]** and create a social world of their own. That obviously **involved dissociating the week from nature** and its rhythms. **Only by being based on an entirely artificial**

111

mathematical rhythm could the Sabbath observance become totally independent of the lunar or any other natural cycle.

"*The Jewish and astrological weeks evolved quite independently of one another. However, given the coincidence of their identical length, it was only a matter of time before some permanent correspondence between particular Jewish days and particular planetary days would be made.*

CATHOLIC ENCYCLOPEDIA

CALENDAR

*In the Roman chronological system of the Augustan age the week as a division of time was practically unknown, though the twelve calendar months existed as we have them now. In the course of the first and second century after Christ, the hebdomadal or seven-day period became universally familiar, though not immediately through Jewish or Christian influence. The arrangement seems to have been astrological in origin and to have come to Rome from Egypt. The seven planets, as then conceived of-- Saturn, Jupiter, Mars, the Sun, Venus, Mercury, and the Moon, thus arranged in the order of their periodic times (Saturn taking the longest and the Moon the shortest time to complete the round of the heavens by their proper motion)-- were supposed to preside over each hour successively, **and the day was designated by that planet which presided over its first hour. Beginning on the first day with the planets in order, the first hour would be Saturn's,** the second Jupiter's, the seventh the Moon's, the eighth Saturn's again, and so on.*

SUN-WORSHIP AND THE ORIGIN OF SUNDAY

Samuele Bacchiocchi, Ph. D., Andrews University

The existence and common use of the planetary week already in the first century A.D. are well attested by several testimonies. In the present study we need refer only to few of them. The Roman historian Dio Cassius, who wrote his Roman History between A.D. 200-220, reports that Jerusalem was captured both by Pompey in 63 B.C. and by Gaius Sosius in 37 B.C. "on the day even then called the day of Saturn." That the praxis of naming the days of the week after the planetary deities was already in use before Christ is further corroborated by the contemporary references of Horace (ca. 35 B.C.) to "dies Jovis— Thursday" and of Tibullus (ca. B.C. 29-30) to dies Saturni—Saturday." Dio Cassius himself speaks of the planetary week as "prevailing everywhere" in his time to the extent that among the Romans it was "already an ancestral custom."

Two Sabine calendars found in central Italy in 1795 and a third one which came to light at Cimitele, near Nola in southern Italy, in 1956 (**all three dated no later than the time of Tiberius (A.D. 14-37), present in the right column the eight letters from A to H of the eight-day Roman nundinum market week** and in the left column the seven letters from A to G, representing the seven-day planetary week. In addition to these calendars should be considered also several so-called "indices nundinarii" (some of them dated in the early empire). These give the name of the towns **and the corresponding days of the planetary week (which** *always starts with Saturday—dies Saturni) on which the market was to be held.*

NOTE: The following quotes are harder to understand, but definitely moon based talk!

PHILO

ON MATING XIX

*For it is said in the scripture: "On the tenth day of this month let each of them take a sheep according to his house; {23}{#ex 12:3.} in order that from the tenth, there may be consecrated to the tenth, that is to God, the sacrifices which have been preserved in the soul, which is illuminated in two portions out of the three, until it is entirely changed in every part, and becomes a heavenly brilliancy **like a full moon, at the height of its increase at the end of the second week,***

NOTE: Philo is comparing the glory of the lamb sacrifice to the full moon. Isn't it a curious statement for him to make as to the full moon being at the end of the 2nd week? (The full moon IS in the middle of the lunar month AND at the end of the second lunar week).

ALLEGORICAL INTERPRETATION I - IV

But nature delights in the number seven, for there are seven planets, going in continual opposition to the daily course of the heaven which always proceeds in the same direction. And likewise the constellation of the Bear is made up of seven stars, which constellation is the cause of communication and unity among men, and not merely of traffic. Again, the periodical changes of the moon, take

114

place according to the number seven, that star having the greatest sympathy with the things on earth. And the changes which the moon works in the air, it perfects chiefly in accordance with its own configurations on each seventh day.

XXX. (161) But to the seventh day of the week he has assigned the greatest festivals, those of the longest duration, at the periods of the equinox both vernal and autumnal in each year; appointing two festivals for these two epochs, each lasting seven days; the one which takes place in the spring being for the perfection of what is being sown, and the one which falls in autumn being a feast of thanksgiving for the bringing home of all the fruits which the trees have produced. And seven days have very appropriately been appointed to the seventh month of each equinox, so that **each month** might receive **an especial honour of one sacred day of festival**, for the purpose of refreshing and cheering the mind with its holiday.

(155) And this feast is **begun on the fifteenth day of the month,** in the middle of the month, **on the day on which the moon is full of light,** in consequence of the providence of God taking care that there shall be no darkness on that day.

JOSEPHUS

ANTIQUITIES OF THE JEWS... BOOK 3, CH.10

5. In the month of Xanthicus, which is by us called Nisan, and is the beginning of our year, on **the fourteenth day of the lunar month,** when the sun is in Aries, (for in this month it was that we were delivered from bondage under the Egyptians,) the law ordained that we should every year slay that sacrifice which I before told you we slew when we

came out of Egypt, and which was called the Passover; and so we do celebrate this Passover in companies, leaving nothing of what we sacrifice till the day following. **The feast of unleavened bread succeeds that of the Passover, and falls on the fifteenth day of the month,** *and continues seven days, wherein they feed on unleavened bread; on every one of which days two bulls are killed, and one ram, and seven lambs. Now these lambs are entirely burnt, besides the kid of the goats which is added to all the rest, for sins; for it is intended as a feast for the priest on every one of those days. But on the* **second day of unleavened bread, which is the sixteenth day of the month, they first partake of the fruits of the earth, for before that day they do not touch them.** *And while they suppose it proper to honor God, from whom they obtain this plentiful provision, in the first place, they offer the first-fruits of their barley, and that in the manner following: They take a handful of the ears, and dry them, then beat them small, and purge the barley from the bran; they then bring one tenth deal to the altar, to God; and, casting one handful of it upon the fire, they leave the rest for the use of the priest. And after this it is that they may publicly or privately reap their harvest. They also at this participation of the first-fruits of the earth, sacrifice a lamb, as a burnt-offering to God.*

MISHNA

ROSH-HASHSHANA

4:3 In olden times the lulab{lulab The branches of palm, myrtle, and willow which are bound together and carried along with the etrog on the Festival of Booths Lev. 23:40.} was taken up in the Temple for seven days, and in the provinces, for one day. `When the Temple was destroyed,

Rabban Yohanan ben Zakkai made the rule that in the provinces the lulab{lulab The branches of palm, myrtle, and willow which are bound together and carried along with the etrog on the Festival of Booths Lev. 23:40.} should be taken up for seven days, as a memorial to the Temple; `**and that the day [the sixteenth of Nisan]** on which the omer{omer The first sheaf of the season, which must be harvested and offered in the Temple as a meal offering. Only when this is done may the rest of the new grain be reaped Lev. 23: 10.} is waved should be wholly prohibited [in regard to the eating of new produce] [M. eSuk. 3:12].

Lev 23:11 And he shall wave the sheaf before the LORD, to be accepted for you; **on the morrow after the Sabbath the priest shall wave it.**

Lev 23:14 And ye shall eat neither bread, nor parched corn, nor fresh ears, **until this selfsame day,** until ye have brought the offering of your God; it is a statute forever throughout your generations in all your dwellings.

POLYCRATES, BISHOP OF EPHESUS

VOL 8.0 8.10

[a.d. 130-196.] This author comes in as an appendix to the stories of Polycarp and Irenæus and good Anicetus, and his writings also bear upon the contrast presented by the less creditable history of Victor. If, as I suppose, the appearance of our Lord to St. John on "the Lord's day" was on the Paschal Sunday, it may at first seem surprising that this Apostle can be claimed by Polycrates in behalf of the Eastern custom to keep Easter, with the Jews, on the fourteenth day of the moon. But to the Jews **the Apostles** *became "as Jews" in all things tolerable, **so long as the Temple stood, and while the bishops of Jerusalem** were labouring to identify the Paschal Lamb with their Passover. **The long survival of St. John among Jewish Christians led them to prolong this usage, no doubt, as sanctioned by his example. He foreknew it would quietly pass away.** The wise and truly Christian spirit of Irenæus prepared the way for the ultimate unanimity of the Church in a matter which lies at the base of "the Christian Sabbath," and of our own observance of the first day of the week as a weekly Easter. **Those who in our own times have revived the observance of the Jewish Sabbath,** show us how much may be said on their side, and elucidate the tenacity of the Easterns in resisting the abolition of the Mosaic ordinance as to the Paschal, although they agreed to keep it "not with the old leaven."*

ANATOLIUS

(230-280 AD) VOL 6.04.02

*"There is, then, in the first year, **the new moon of the first month**, which is the beginning of every cycle of nineteen years, **on the six and twentieth day of the month called by the Egyptians Phamenoth.** But, **according to the months of the Macedonians, it is on the two-and-twentieth day of Dystrus.** And, **as the Romans would say, it is on the eleventh day before the Kalends of April.** Now the sun is found on the said six-and-twentieth day of Phamenoth, not only as having mounted to the first segment, but as already passing the fourth day in it. And this segment they are accustomed to call the first dodecatemorion (twelfth part), and the equinox, and the beginning of months, and the head of the cycle, and the starting-point of the course of the planets. And the segment before this they call the last of the*

months, and the twelfth segment, and the last dodecatemorion, and the end of the circuit of the planets. And for this reason, also, we maintain that those who place the first month in it, and who determine the fourteenth day of the Paschal season by it, make no trivial or common blunder."

"Nor is this an opinion confined to ourselves alone. For it was also known to the Jews of old and before Christ, and it was most carefully observed by them. And this may be learned from what Philo, and Josephus, and Musaeus have written;"

"But nothing was difficult to them with whom it was lawful to celebrate the Passover on any day when the fourteenth of the moon happened after the equinox. Following their example up to the present time all the bishops of Asia - as themselves also receiving the rule from an unimpeachable authority, to wit, the evangelist John, who leant on the Lord's breast, and drank in instructions spiritual without doubt - **were in the way of celebrating the Paschal feast, without question, every year, whenever the fourteenth day of the moon had come, and the lamb was sacrificed by the Jews after the equinox was past;** not acquiescing, so far as regards this matter, with the authority of some, namely, the successors of Peter and Paul, who have taught all the churches in which they sowed the spiritual seeds of the Gospel, that the solemn festival of the resurrection of the Lord can be celebrated only on the Lord's day. **Whence, also, a certain contention broke out between the successors of these, namely, Victor, at that time bishop of the city of Rome, and Polycrates, who then appeared to hold the primacy among the bishops of Asia.** And this contention was adjusted most rightfully by Irenaeus, at that time president of a part of Gaul, so that *both parties kept by their own order, and did not decline from the original custom of antiquity.* **The one party, (Polycrates) indeed, kept the Paschal day on the fourteenth day of the first month, according to the Gospel, as they thought, adding nothing of an extraneous kind, but keeping through all things the rule of faith.** *And the other party, passing the day of the Lord's Passion as one replete with sadness and grief, hold that it should not be lawful to celebrate the Lord's mystery of the Passover at any other time but on the Lord's day, on which the resurrection of the Lord from death took place, and on which rose also for us the cause of everlasting joy."*

CLEMENT OF ALEXANDRIA

VOL 2.05.03

"And the paschal feast **began with the tenth day**, *being the transition from all trouble, and from all objects of sense."*

EPIPHANIUS

(PANARION -BOOK II AND BOOK III) 310-403 AD

(2) For they choose to celebrate the Passover with the Jews – that is, they contentiously celebrate the Passover at the same time that the Jews are holding their Festival of Unleavened Bread. **And indeed, <it is true> that this used to be the church's custom -**

(9) For long ago even from the earliest days, its various celebrations in the church differed – (8) And in a word, as is not unknown to many scholarly persons, there was a lot of muddle and tiresomeness every time a controversy was

120

aroused in the church's teaching about this festival....and down to our own day. **This has been the situation ever since <the church> was thrown into disorder after the time of the circumcised bishops.**

(4) And there were altogether fifteen bishops from the circumcision. And at that time, when the circumcised bishops were consecrated at Jerusalem, **it was essential that the whole world follow and celebrate with them.** *<But> since <the festival> could not be celebrated <in this way> for such a long time, by God's good pleasure <a* **correction> was made for harmony's sake in the time of Constantine.**

12,1 And much could be said about the good the fathers did – or rather, the good God did through them – by arriving at the absolutely correct determination, for the church, of this all-venerable, all-holy Paschal Feast, its celebration after the equinox, which is the day on which the date of the fourteenth of the lunar month falls. Not that we are to keep it on the fourteenth itself; the Jews require one day while we require not one day but six, a full week. (2)The Law itself says, to extend the time, **"Ye shall take for yourselves a lamb** *of a year old, without blemish perfect,* **on the tenth of the month***, and ye shall keep it until the fourteenth, and ye shall slay it near evening on the fourteenth day of the month that is, the lunar. But the church observes the Paschal festival,* **that is, the week which is designated even by the apostles themselves in the Ordinance, beginning with the second day of the week, the purchase of the lamb.** *And the lamb is publicly slaughtered (i.e. by the Jews)*

NOTE: If you look closely at the underlined quote in the last paragraph of Epiphanius, he makes a statement from the Ordinance of the apostles about **beginning on the second day of the week – the purchase of the lamb.** He then goes into this confusing Passover explanation of how to fit the six required days they kept at that time by using the Julian calendar. However, that statement by the apostles is based on a lunar week, for on the lunar calendar the 10th of the month IS the second day of the week. This statement is also made above by Clement of Alexandria right before Epiphanius.

TWO PERPETUAL CALENDARS
BY WILLIAM BECKER 1995

The inconsistencies of the present calendar came about by the forced amalgamation (by Constantine) of the Roman (Egyptian) solar calendar of 365 (or 366) days, with the 28-day lunar calendar divided into quarters of seven-day weeks. The calendar as we know it repeats the same date on the same day of the month and week only after several years, as I'm sure you are aware. Grasshopper Dates.

The problem is to make the solar year divisible into seven-day lunar weeks, which are now so ingrained into our way of life. Three hundred and sixty four days divided by seven equals 52 weeks.

SAMUELE BACCHIOCCHI, PD
ANDREWS UNIVERSITY

Even the strictest Jewish sects objected to fasting on the Sabbath. The rabbis, though they differed in their views regarding the time and number of the Sabbath meals, *agreed that food on the Sabbath ought to be abundant and good. The following statement epitomizes perhaps the typical rabbinic view: "Do you think that I (God) gave you the Sabbath as burden? I gave it to you for your benefit.' How? Explained Rabbi Hiyya bar Abba **(180-230 a.d.)**, 'Keep the Sabbath holy with food, drink and clean garment, enjoy yourself and I shall reward you."*

NOTE: They could not have the Sabbath and Yom Kippur land on the same day for this Rabbi to make such a statement. Fast or feast was not a thought at the time of this quote (180-230a.d.).

EVIDENCE OF THE CRESENT AS YHWH'S WAY

THE INTERNATIONAL STANDARD BIBLE ENCYCLOPEDIA *(1844-1913)*

PHASES OF THE MOON.

There is no direct mention of the phases of the moon in Scripture; a remarkable fact, **and one that illustrates the foolishness of attempting to prove the ignorance of the sacred writers by the argument from silence, since it is not conceivable that men at any time were ignorant of the fact that the moon changes her apparent shape and size.** So far from the Hebrews being plunged in such a depth of more than savage ignorance, **they based their whole calendar on the actual observation of the first appearance of the young crescent.** In two passages in the Revised Version (British and American) we find the expression "at the full moon," keceh (Ps 81:3; Pr 7:20), but though this is what is intended, the literal meaning of the word is doubtful, and may be that given in the King James Version, "at the day appointed." In another passage already quoted, there is a reference to the dark part of the month. "Thy sun shall no more go down, neither shall thy moon (yerach, "month") withdraw itself"--the "withdrawn" part of the month being the time near new moon when the moon is nearly in conjunction with the sun and therefore invisible.

The moon indicated the time for monthly worship; **when the slender crescent of the new moon was first seen in the western sky,** special sacrifices were ordained with the blowing of trumpets over them.

ENCYCLOPEDIA JUDAICA

"Originally, the New Moon was not fixed by astronomical calculation, but was solemnly proclaimed after witnesses had testified to the **reappearance of the crescent of the moon**," ...**The switchover** from watching for the first visible crescent **to calculating conjunctions** to determine the month's beginning came with Hillel II's calendar revisions **in the 4th century A.D**. "By the middle of the fourth century, the sages had established a permanent calendar and the public proclamation of the New Moon was discontinued"

ENCYCLOPEDIA BIBLICA

The **appearance of the new moon** inaugurated a new period, a new month.... The mean length of such a month is 29d 12h 44m 2.82s, and accordingly it was impossible that the determination of the month, as long as it rested on direct observation only, could arrive at any absolutely uniform result; the observed months inevitably varied in length between 29 and 30 days, and the order in which the months alternated had not yet been fixed even at the time when the Mishna was composed; even at that late date, **in the second century A.D**. the point was **decided by the first visibility of the new moon**.

In later Judaism, the punctual celebration of the day depended on direct observation of the moon itself. Great care was expended in ascertaining **with precision the first visibility of the moon.** The synedrium assembled in the early morning of the 30th day of each month.....till the time of the evening sacrifice. **Whoever first saw the crescent moon** was bound to let the synedrium know of it at once, **it was not till some two centuries after the destruction of the temple** that the Jews began to reckon the new moon by astronomy.

RABBI SAMSON RAPHAEL HIRSCH

The 19th-century German scholar noted that since we would soon be liberated from slavery, **we could appreciate the moon's emergence from darkness to light.** *Through the moon's renewal, God is telling the people of Israel: "This is to be the model for your own conduct!* **Even as the moon renews itself by the law of nature, so you, too, should renew yourselves, but of your own free will."** *God also commanded us to count the months, so that we could always calculate the amount of time that our people have been free.*

ENOCH

CHAPTER LXXIII.

And after this law I saw another law dealing with the smaller luminary, which is named the Moon. 2. And her circumference is like the circumference of the heaven, and her chariot in which she rides is driven by the wind, and light is given to her in (definite) measure. 3. And her rising and setting change every month: and her days are like the days of the sun, and when her light is uniform (i.e. full) it amounts to the seventh part of the light of the sun. 4. And thus she rises. **and her first phase in the east comes forth on the thirtieth morning: and on that day she becomes visible, and constitutes for you the first phase of the moon** *on the thirtieth day together with the sun in the portal where the sunrises.*

CHAPTER LXXVII.

5. And they set and enter the portals of the west, and make their revolution by the north, and come forth through the eastern portals on the face of the heaven. 6. **And when**

the moon rises one-fourteenth part appears in the heaven:
/the light becomes full in her /: on the fourteenth day she
accomplishes her light. 7. And fifteen parts of light are
transferred to her till the fifteenth day (when) her light is
accomplished, according to the sign of the year, and she
becomes fifteen parts, and the moon grows by (the addition
of) fourteenth parts. 8. And in her waning (the moon)
decreases on the first day to fourteen parts of her light, on
the second to thirteen parts of light, on the third to twelve,
on the fourth to eleven, on the fifth to ten, on the sixth to
nine, on the seventh to eight, on the eighth to seven, on the
ninth to six, on the tenth to five, on the eleventh to four, on
the twelfth to three, on the thirteenth to two, on the
fourteenth to the half of a seventh, and all her remaining
light disappears wholly on the fifteenth. 9. And in certain
months the month has twenty-nine days and once twenty-
eight. 10. And Uriel showed me another law: when light is
transferred to the moon, and on which side it is transferred
to her by the sun. 11. During all the period during which
the moon is growing in her light, she is transferring it to
herself when opposite to the sun during fourteen days [her
light is accomplished in the heaven], and when she is
illumined throughout, her light is accomplished full in the
*heaven. 12. **And on the first day she is called the new***
***moon, for on that day the light rises upon her.** 13. She*
becomes full moon exactly on the day when the sun sets in
the west, and from the east she rises at night, and the moon
shines the whole night through till the sun rises over against
her and the moon is seen over against the sun. 14. On the
*side whence the light of the moon comes forth, **there again***
she wanes till all the light vanishes and all the days of the
month are at an end, and her circumference is empty, void
of light.

NOTE: There is no doubt here in Enoch that the first visible crescent points to the beginning of the month and the dark moon is the end.

CHRONOLOGICAL AND GEOGRAPHIC BASIS OF THE HISTORY OF JESUS CHRIST
p.5, Section 7

*"The month of the Jews was, as we have said, a lunar month, and extended **from one appearing of the new moon to another**. The time elapsing between one astronomical new moon and another consists of 29.5 days. . . But since the month consisted of entire days, they counted it with pretty regular alternation as 29 or 30 days. A month of 30 days was called a full month . . . if it had only 29 days, it was called an imperfect month . . . The Jewish month could never have more than 30 days, and never fewer than 29. **It began, not with the astronomical new moon, but with the new light; that is to say, when the first light of the renewed phase of the moon became visible."***

HILLEL.ORG WEBSITE

*"The calendar is so central to Judaism that it is the first commandment the Jews were given as a nation... The lunar month begins at the exact moment when the moon begins its new cycle. At this precise moment the moon is lined up with the sun and earth in such a way that it is completely invisible. This moment is called the molad, or "birth" of the new moon; **however, the Jewish month was not originally calculated from the molad.** Rather, the Rabbis point to the verse, "This month" which implies that there was **something***

*tangible for Moses to see. **They teach that the new month begins with the appearance of the new crescent, which is AFTER the molad.** When the Sanhedrin, or Supreme Court, convened, the new month could be established only by the Sanhedrin based on the testimony of two witnesses who were able to **verify that they had seen** the new moon.*

*This biblical Hebrew word 'hodesh' refers, as it does in later Hebrew, to **the first visible crescent of the waxing moon**, which is **the starting point** of the moon's visible changes throughout the sky.*

DR. JULIAN OBERMANN
Jewish Professor of Semitic Languages at Yale University

*"However, it is very important to recognize that the progression of the moladim **does not usually coincide exactly with the lunar conjunction,** (nor with any phase of the moon). There are two elements of this disparity: **The calculated molad is based upon a constant period of time**, approximating a mean average of the lunation; **however, the duration of the actual lunation varies from month to month.***

FULL MOON CYCLE, WIKIPEDIA, THE FREE ENCYCLOPEDIA

PERIODIC CORRECTIONS
The Moon's *phases* do not repeat very regularly: the time between two similar syzygies may vary between 29.272 and 29.833 days. The reason is that the orbit of the Moon is elliptic, its velocity is not constant, so the

time of the true syzygy will differ from the mean syzygy.

WHAT ABOUT THE BEGINNING OF A DAY?

ENCYCLOPEDIA BIBLICA

DAY VOL. I p.554

From **dawn to dark was the ancient and ordinary meaning** of a day (yome) among the Israelites; night as being the time 'when no man can work' (Jn. 9:4), night, it was considered, be left out of account altogether, or, at all events, as being the evident complement of the 'day' and involved in it, did not require explicit mention. Thus the word 'day' came to have a twofold meaning: at one time signifying **the period from sunrise to sunset**; at another including day's inseparable accompaniment, the night, and embracing the whole **period from one sunrise to the next.**

The Israelites regarded the morning as the beginning of the day;...

Not till post-exilic times do we find traces of a new mode of reckoning **which makes day begin at sunset.**

THE JEWISH FESTIVALS: HISTORY AND OBSERVANCE

"In order **to assure against profanation** of the Sabbath the **Jews added the late Friday afternoon** hours to the Sabbath." p.13

JUDAISM: BETWEEN YESTERDAY AND TOMORROW   KUNG, p.518

"If we look at the essentials of a day of rest and reflection which has a religious orientation, **it is possible to justify** the **shifting of the Sabbath worship to Friday evening** [the celebration of which was **moved back to the eve of the feast**] as early as the Middle Ages."

JEWISH ENCYCLOPEDIA

p. 591-597

"**In order to fix the beginning and ending of the Sabbath-day and festivals** and to determine the precise hour for certain religious observances it becomes necessary to know the exact times of the rising and setting of the sun. According to the strict interpretation of the Mosaic Law, **every day begins with sunrise and ends with sunset**..."

DAY p.475
(Hebrew, "yom"): in the bible, the season of light (Gen. 1:5), lasting "from **dawn (lit. "the rising of the morning")** to the coming forth of the stars"

JACOB Z. LAUTERBACH, "THE SABBATH IN JEWISH RITUAL AND FOLKLORE,"
"Rabbinic Essays by Jacob Z. Lauterbach," (Hebrew Union College Press, Cincinnati, 1951), p.437-470

WHEN DOES THE SABBATH BEGIN?
There can be no doubt that in pre-exilic times the Israelites reckoned the **day from morning to morning.** The

day began with the dawn and closed with the end of the night following it, i.e. with the last moment before the dawn of the next morning..."And it was evening and it was morning, one day." **THIS PASSAGE WAS MISUNDERSTOOD BY THE TALMUD**, *... But it was correctly interpreted by R. Samuel b. Meir (1100-1160) when he remarked:* **"It does not say that it was night time and it was day time which made one day;** *but it says* **'it was evening,' which means that the period of the day time came to an end and the light disappeared.** *And when it* **says 'it was morning,' it means that the period of the night time came to an end and the morning dawned.** *Then one whole day was completed*

JULIAN MORGENSTERN,
"THE SOURCES OF THE CREATION STORY
Gen. 1:1-2:4," AJSL, XXXVI, (The University of Chicago Press, Chicago, 1920), p.169-212

In early Jewish practice, ..., **it seems to have been customary to reckon the day from sunrise to sunrise, or, rather, from dawn to dawn.** *Thus the law for the "praise-offering" (Lev. 7:17 [Pt]) specifies that this sacrifice must be eaten on the day upon which it is offered, and that nothing may be left until morning. The repetition of the law in Lev. 22:30... is even more explicit: "On that very day (when it was sacrificed) it shall be eaten; ye shall not leave anything of it until morning.* **Clearly the next morning is here reckoned as belonging to the next day, and not the same day** *as the preceding evening and night.* **In other words, the day is reckoned here from sunrise to sunrise.**

"THE TORAH - A MODERN COMMENTARY,"
Gunther Plaut, (Union of American Hebrew Congregations, NY, 1981), p.920- 930

'At what point did the civil day begin? **There is some evidence that at one time the day was reckoned from sunrise to sunrise.** But before the close of the biblical period, it had become standard to reckon the day from sunset to sunset, and this has been Jewish practice ever since...

ISMAR SCHORSCH, 5758 PARASHAH 'BERESHIT'
(Chancellor of the Jewish Theological Seminary, New York)

"Six times the opening chapter of the Torah repeats the poetic refrain 'and there was evening and there was morning', to signal the completion of a divine day's work. The Torah seems to be going out of its way to establish the fact that the day does not begin with the crack of dawn, but rather with the setting of the sun...But is this what the oft-repeated phrase actually means? **Not according to the grandson of Rashi**, Rabbi Samuel ben Meir...he noted that the Torah spoke of 'evening' and not 'night'...Modern Jewish commentators have tended to confirm and amplify this independent insight of Samuel ben Meir **by pointing out that throughout the Bible the unit of a day actually starts with the morning**...in fact, toward the end of his life, **Rashi confessed to his grandson** that if he were to compose his own biblical commentary afresh, he (Rashi) would be even more attentive to the peshat than he had been...**Where a specific religious observance has been abandoned by the** *people, no amount of exegetical authoritarianism can revive it... WE MAY NEVER KNOW WHAT PROMPTED THE RABBIS TO RECONFIGURE THE DAY..."*

NOTE: I have copied quotes from 34 different sources for supporting a lunar based Sabbath, 9 sources for the first sliver crescent being the beginning of the new month, and 8 sources for when a day begins which, by the way, goes way beyond the two to three witnesses needed. If I were to continue digging I am sure I could find more. If this was *not* such a common way to follow the days of the month, by lunar/solar ways, then it would *not* be something constantly brought up historically. I repeat; there are conflicting explanations how to figure the weeks in a lunar calendar, however if you along with someone else knew nothing about putting a wagon harness on a horse and hitching it up and you were given one to do just that – most likely you would not agree on how all the straps go on. However, give it to an Amish farmer and voila! There you have it. It takes time and study and practice to get it right. This was not an event; *it was a process* which started after the destruction of the temple. The fact of the matter is that even though agreement among the different writers is lacking on exactly when this happened; it still remains that just like the unearthed bones, **they agreed that it *DID* happen**. I guess the big question is: Are we going to continue to strain at the gnats and swallow the camel or are we going to ask the important question – *why is this subject even talked about by all these writers if it didn't exist at all?*

APPENDIX A

MATTHEW 12:40 - UNDER THE MICROSCOPE

This subject seems to me to have taken on a life of its own; causing more confusion about the truth of the matter of how long Yeshua was **in the grave** and when he rose from the dead.

I feel we must thoroughly examine all scripture on this matter to try to see the true message and connection with the Spring Feasts; Passover, Unleavened bread and First Fruits.

Let us first lay the ground work for judging a matter.

*Deu 17:6 **At the mouth of two witnesses, or three witnesses**, shall he that is worthy of death be put to death; but at the mouth of one witness he shall not be put to death.*

*Deu 19:15 **One witness shall not rise up against a man** for any iniquity, or for any sin, in any sin that he sinneth: **at the mouth of two witnesses, or at the mouth of three witnesses, shall the matter be established**.*

*Joh 5:31 **"If I testify about myself, my testimony is not true**. 32 There is another who testifies about me, and I know that the testimony he gives about me is true.*

*Joh 8:17 In your own law it is written that **the testimony of two people is valid.** 18 I am testifying about myself, and the Father who sent me is testifying about me."*

NOTE: By these verses above, a matter needs at least two witnesses to be valid. In the gospels, what does Yeshua say about His death?

*Mat 16:21 From that time forth began Yeshua to shew unto his disciples, how that he must go unto Jerusalem, and suffer many things of the elders and chief priests and scribes, and be killed, and **be raised again the third day.***

*Mat 17:23 And they shall kill him, and **the third day he shall be raised again**. And they were exceeding sorry.*

Mat 20:18 Behold, we go up to Jerusalem; and the Son of man shall be betrayed unto the chief priests and unto the scribes, and they shall condemn him to death, 19 And shall *deliver him to the Gentiles to mock, and to scourge, and to crucify him: and **the third day he shall rise again**.*

*Mar 8:31 And he began to teach them, that the Son of man must suffer many things, and be rejected of the elders, and of the chief priests, and scribes, and be killed, and **after three days rise again.***

NOTE: The word translated 'after' could also have been translated 'in, on, against, upon.

*Mar 9:31 For he taught his disciples, and said unto them, The Son of man is delivered into the hands of men, and they shall kill him; and after that he is killed, **he shall rise the third day.***

*Mar 10:33 Saying, Behold, we go up to Jerusalem; and the Son of man shall be delivered unto the chief priests, and unto the scribes; and they shall condemn him to death, and shall deliver him to the Gentiles: 34 And they shall mock him, and shall scourge him, and shall spit upon him, and shall kill him: and **the third day he shall rise again.***

*Luk 9:20 He said unto them, But whom say ye that I am? Peter answering said, The Messiah of YHVH. 21 And he straitly charged them, and commanded them to tell no man that thing; 22 Saying, The Son of man must suffer many things, and be rejected of the elders and chief priests and scribes, and be slain, and **be raised the third day.***

*Joh 2:18 Then answered the Jews and said unto him, What sign shewest thou unto us, seeing that thou doest these things? 19 Yeshua answered and said unto them, "Destroy this temple, **and in three days I will raise it up"**. 20 Then said the Jews, Forty and six years was this temple in* *building,* **and wilt thou rear it up in three days?** *21 But he spake of the temple of his body. 22 When therefore he was risen from the dead, his disciples remembered that he had said this unto them; and they believed the scripture, and the word which Yeshua had said.*

Luk 24:45 *Then opened he their understanding, that they might understand the scriptures, 46 And said unto them, Thus it is written, and thus it behoved the Messiah to suffer,* and **to rise from the dead the third day:**

Above we have nine times Yeshua proclaimed the time of His rising from the grave. That is **nine** witnesses! How did the people understand what he meant?

Mat 26:59 *Now the chief priests, and elders, and all the council, sought false witness against Yeshua, to put him to death; 60 But found none: yea, though many false witnesses came, yet found they none. At the last came two false witnesses, 61 And said, This fellow said, I am able to destroy the temple of Elohim, and to build it* **in three days.**

Mat 27:39 *And they that passed by reviled him, wagging their heads, 40 And saying, Thou that destroyest the temple, and buildest it* **in three days**, *save thyself. If thou be the Son of Elohim, come down from the cross.*

Mat 27:62 *Now the next day, that followed the day of the preparation, the chief priests and Pharisees came together unto Pilate, 63 Saying, Sir, we remember that that deceiver said, while he was yet alive,* **After three days I will rise again.** *64 Command therefore that the sepulchre be made sure* **until the third day**, *lest his disciples come by night,* *and steal him away, and say unto the people, He is risen from the dead: so the last error shall be worse than the first.*

NOTE: Look above at Mar 8:31. If it really meant 'after' why the statement in the next verse UNTIL the third day? Shouldn't it say until the fourth day?

*Mar 14:58 We heard him say, I will destroy this temple that is made with hands, and **within three days** I will build another made without hands.*

*Mar 15:29 And they that passed by railed on him, wagging their heads, and saying, Ah, thou that destroyest the temple, and buildest it **in three days,***

*Luk 24:5 And as they were afraid, and bowed down their faces to the earth, they said unto them, Why seek ye the living among the dead? 6 He is not here, **but is risen**: remember how he spake unto you when he was yet in Galilee, 7 Saying, The Son of man must be delivered into the hands of sinful men, and be crucified, and **the third day rise again.***

NOTE: Even the Angels are proclaiming it is the third day.

*Luk 24:12 **Then arose Peter, and ran unto the sepulchre**; and stooping down, he beheld the linen clothes laid by themselves, and departed, wondering in himself at that which was come to pass. 13 And**, behold, two of them went that same day to a village called Emmaus,** which was from Jerusalem about threescore furlongs. 14 And they talked together of all these things which had happened. 15 And it came to pass, that, while they communed together*

140

*and reasoned, Yeshua himself drew near, and went with them. 16 But their eyes were holden that they should not know him. 17 And he said unto them, What manner of communications are these that ye have one to another, as ye walk, and are sad? 18 And the one of them, whose name was Cleopas, answering said unto him, Art thou only a stranger in Jerusalem, and hast not known the things which are come to pass therein these days? 19 And he said unto them, What things? And they said unto him, Concerning Yeshua of Nazareth, which was a prophet mighty in deed and word before Elohim and all the people: 20 And **how the chief priests and our rulers delivered him to be condemned to death, and have crucified him.** 21 But we trusted that it had been he which should have redeemed Israel: and beside all this, **today is the third day since these things were done.** 22 Yea, and certain women also of our company made us astonished, which were early at the sepulchre; **23** And when they found not his body, they came, saying, that they had also seen a vision of angels, which said that he was alive.*

I think this last proclamation of the events is the most solid proof of the timing of the days of Yeshua's trial, crucifixion, burial and resurrection. Where else can we look for evidence of the sequence of the days?

*Joh 19:13 When Pilate therefore heard that saying, he brought Yeshua forth, and sat down in the judgment seat in a place that is called the Pavement, but in the Hebrew, Gabbatha. 14 **And it was the preparation of the passover, and about the sixth hour:** and he saith unto the Jews, Behold your King!*

*Mar 15:42 And now when the even was come, **because it was the preparation,** that is, **the day before the sabbath,** 43 Joseph of Arimathaea, and honourable counsellor, which also waited for the kingdom of YHVH, came, and went in boldly unto Pilate, and craved the body of Yeshua.*

*Luk 23:52 This man went unto Pilate, and begged the body of Yeshua. 53 And he took it down, and wrapped it in linen, and laid it in a sepulchre that was hewn in stone, wherein never man before was laid. 54 **And that day was the preparation, and the sabbath drew on.***

NOTE: The meaning of 'drew on' is 'to grow light'

*Joh 19:31 The Jews therefore, **because it was the preparation,** that the bodies **should not remain upon the stake on the sabbath day,** (for that sabbath day was an high day,)besought Pilate that their legs might be broken, and that they might be taken away.*

NOTE: 'high day' is more correctly translated 'great'. It was still THE Sabbath.

*Joh 19:40 Then took they the body of Yeshua, and wound it in linen clothes with the spices, as the manner of the Jews is to bury. 41 Now in the place where he was crucified there was a garden; and in the garden a new sepulchre, wherein was never man yet laid. 42 There laid they Yeshua therefore **because of the Jews preparation day;** for the sepulchre was nigh at hand.*

*Luk 24:1 Now upon **the first day of the week,** very early in the morning, they came unto the sepulchre, bringing the spices which they had prepared, and certain others with* them. 2 And they found the stone rolled away from the sepulchre.

Joh 20:1 On the first day of the week, early in the morning and while it was still dark, Mary Magdalene went to the tomb and noticed that the stone had been removed from the tomb…………Joh 20:18 Mary Magdalene came and told the disciples that she had seen Yeshua, and that he had spoken these things unto her. 19 Then **the same day at evening, being the first day of the week**, when the doors were shut where the disciples were assembled for fear of the Jews, came Yeshua and stood in the midst, and saith unto them, Peace be unto you.

Mar 15:47 And Mary Magdalene and Mary the mother of Joses **beheld where he was laid**.

Mar 16:1 And when the sabbath was past, Mary Magdalene, and Mary the mother of James, and Salome, had bought sweet spices, that they might come and anoint him. 2 And **very early in the morning the first day of the week,** they came unto the sepulchre at the rising of the sun.

Mar 16:9 Now **when Yeshua was risen early the first day of the week**, he appeared first to Mary Magdalene,

Luk 23:55 And the women also, which came with him from Galilee, followed after, and **beheld the sepulchre, and how his body was laid. 56 And they returned, and prepared spices and ointments;** and **rested the sabbath day according to the commandment.**

Okay, so we have the trial and crucifixion on the preparation day which included the meal of Passover and for the Sabbath the next day. He is laid in the tomb that evening, the women note His burial place and go home for Sabbath **(please note that if Sabbath is the 7ᵗʰ day of the week, it is the LAST day of the week).**The *first day* of the new week they go to the tomb and find it empty. Yeshua then meets the two on the road that very day until evening and then appears to His disciples that evening of the THIRD day. Have I overlooked anything? Oh Yeah, the Jonah thing. What is really going on in the verses of Jonah? Have we honestly studied the total proclamation of Yeshua in them? Let's look at the verses now.

Mat 12:38 Then certain of the scribes and of the Pharisees answered, saying, Rabbi, we would see a sign from thee. 39 But he answered and said unto them, An evil and adulterous generation seeketh after a sign; and there shall no sign be given to it, but the sign of the prophet Jonas: 40 For as Jonas was three days and three nights in the whales belly; so shall the Son of man be three days and three nights in the heart of the earth. 41 The men of Nineveh shall rise in judgment with this generation, and shall condemn it: **because they repented at the preaching of Jonas;** *and, behold,* **a greater than Jonas is here.** *42 The queen of the south shall rise up in the judgment with this generation, and shall condemn it: **for she came from the uttermost parts of the earth to hear the wisdom of Solomon;** and, behold, **a greater than Solomon is here.***

*Luk 11:28 But he said, Yea rather, **blessed are they that hear the word of YHVH, and keep it**. 29 And when the people were gathered thick together, he began to say, This*

144

*is an evil generation: they seek a sign; and there shall no sign be given it, but the sign of Jonas the prophet. 30 For as Jonas was a sign unto the Ninevites, so shall also the Son of man be to this generation. 31 The queen of the south shall rise up in the judgment with the men of this generation, and condemn them: **for she came from the utmost parts of the earth to hear the wisdom of Solomon;** and, behold, **a greater than Solomon is here.** 32 The men of Nineve shall rise up in the judgment with this generation, and shall condemn it: **for they repented at the preaching of Jonas;** and, behold, **a greater than Jonas is here.***

When reading these two references, *it is quite obvious Yeshua is talking about hearing Him and obeying His instructions and warnings*; just as the Ninevites heeded the warning of Jonah and the queen of the south listening to the wisdom of Solomon, for these Pharisees and Sadducees had someone even greater with them. This is repeated in two different gospels – *giving at least two witnesses*. I understand that verse 40 in Mathew is the kingpin of problems. Most cannot get past that one to make sense with all the other scriptures of 'in three days' or 'on the third day'. **(Please keep in mind there is only ONE witness in the gospels referring back to Jonah.)**

I do not claim I can explain this verse to everyone's satisfaction, but, I do see through all the accounts of the days taken in the scriptures of Yeshua's Passion, there is no way he was IN the ground even two full days; let alone three. Look – Yeshua died at the 9th hour (3p.m.) on the day of preparation (the 14th), was buried that night as the Sabbath day drew near (grew light). All rested the Sabbath day (the 15th) and early in the morning of the first day (16th) of the week (*remember, the Sabbath is the 7th day of the week; therefore the last day of the week – then comes the first day of the new week*) the women come to an open tomb. He is gone! That does not add up to 3 days and 3 nights in the grave no matter how you cut it. So what could that verse mean? I would like to put forward a possible meaning to this statement. First we need to go back to the Greek definition of a couple of the words in Mat. 12:40.

The word 'heart' – *kardia, (kar-dee'-ah) Prolonged from a primary* κάρ *kar (Latin cor, "heart"); the heart, that is, (figuratively) the thoughts or feelings (mind); also (by analogy) the middle: - (+ broken-) heart (-ed).*

And the word 'earth' - *gē, (ghay) Contracted from a primary word; soil; by extension a region, or the solid part or the whole of the terrene globe (including the occupants in each application): - country, earth (-ly), ground, land, world.*

If you examine these two key words used by Yeshua, could He possibly be saying that His time would **start** with the heart breaking thoughts, feelings and brokenness of what he was sent here to do? Dealing with all the occupants of this world to make a way of redemption? If this makes any sense, please let me continue. Let us now look at the Passover account in John.

Joh 13:1 Now ***before the feast of the passover,*** *when Yeshua knew that his hour was come that he should depart out of this world unto the Father, having loved his own which were in the world, he loved them unto the end. 2* ***And supper being ended,*** *the devil having now put into the heart of Judas Iscariot, Simons son, to betray him;*

Joh 18:1 *When Yeshua had spoken these words,* ***he went forth with his disciples over the brook Cedron, where was a garden, into the which he entered, and his disciples.*** *2 And Judas also, which betrayed him, knew the place: for Yeshua ofttimes resorted thither with his disciples. 3 Judas then, having received a band of men and officers from the chief priests and Pharisees, cometh thither with lanterns and torches and weapons.*

Joh 18:27 ***Peter then denied again: and immediately the cock crew.*** *28 Then led they Yeshua from Caiaphas unto the hall of judgment:* ***and it was early;*** *and* ***they themselves went not into the judgment hall, lest they should be defiled; but that they might eat the passover.*** *29 Pilate then went out unto them, and said, What accusation bring ye against this man?*

Joh 19:13 *When Pilate therefore heard that saying, he brought Yeshua forth, and sat down in the judgment seat in a place that is called the Pavement, but in the Hebrew, Gabbatha. 14* ***And it was the preparation of the passover, and about the sixth hour***: *and he saith unto the Jews, Behold your King!*

Joh 19:30 *When Yeshua therefore had received the vinegar, he said, It is finished: and he bowed his head, and* *gave up the spirit. 31 The Jews therefore,* **because it was the preparation, that the bodies should not remain upon the stake on the sabbath day,** *(for that sabbath day was an high day,)besought Pilate that their legs might be broken, and that they might be taken away.*

Joh 19:40 *Then took they the body of Yeshua, and wound it in linen clothes with the spices, as the manner of the Jews is to bury. 41 Now in the place where he was crucified there was a garden; and in the garden a new sepulchre, wherein was never man yet laid. 42* **There laid they Yeshua therefore because of the Jews preparation day;** *for the sepulchre was nigh at hand.*

Joh 20:1 The first day of the week cometh Mary Magdalene early, *when it was yet dark, unto the sepulchre, and seeth the stone taken away from the sepulchre. 2 Then she runneth, and cometh to Simon Peter, and to the other disciple, whom Yeshua loved, and saith unto them, They have taken away Yeshua out of the sepulchre, and we know not where they have laid him.*

Joh 20:18 *Mary Magdalene came and told the disciples that she had seen Yeshua, and that he had spoken these things unto her. 19* **Then the same day at evening, being the first day of the week,** *when the doors were shut where the disciples were assembled for fear of the Jews, came Yeshua and stood in the midst, and saith unto them, Peace be unto you. 20 And when he had so said, he shewed unto them his hands and his side. Then were the disciples glad, when they saw Yeshua.*

Now let's look at this a little closer. According to John, They ate BEFORE the Passover began. Some ancient writings actually say it was the evening of the 13th. If it were that evening, then after they ate they went to the garden where Yeshua began His labored praying. At about midnight they came and took him to the high priest for the trial. When morning arrived which would be the 14th and the beginning of the preparation day, he was taken to Pilot and then taken to be crucified at the sixth hour of the day; breathed his last at the 9th hour and was taken down that evening, prepared by the two men and laid in a tomb. The next day was the great Sabbath that started the week of unleavened bread and Yeshua (-*By which also he went and preached unto the spirits in prison; 20 Which sometime were disobedient, when once the longsuffering of YHVH waited in the days of Noah, while the ark was a preparing, wherein few, that is, eight souls were saved by water.1Pe 3:19-20)*. The next morning which was the day of First Fruits and the first day of the new week, the women came to the tomb and found it empty! So, what do we have here?

The 13th - in the evening Yeshua had Passover with his disciples and went to the garden – **beginning his agony – night 1.**

The 14th – continued his agony and passion till his death and burial - **Day 1 and night 2.**

Please look at this on the 14th. Here is the fulfilling of the Day of Atonement – evening (13th) to evening (14th) afflicting the soul.

The 15th - The Sabbath and all at rest. **Day 2 and night 3.**

The 16th - The morning of First Fruits, the first day of the week - and the empty tomb. **Day 3.**

(*Co 15:20 But now is the Messiah risen from the dead, **and become the firstfruits of them that slept**. 21 For since by man came death, by man came also the resurrection of the dead. 22 For as in Adam all die, even so in the Messiah shall all be made alive. 23 But every man in his own order: **the Messiah the firstfruits**; afterward they that are the Messiahs at his coming.*)

We must remember that YHWH set up the Feasts – His Feasts – at specific times and on particular days. These were to be shadows for us to follow and watch for His fulfilling of them. He commanded the Israelites to have the Passover on the night of the 14th of Nissan.

*Exo 12:5 Your lamb shall be without blemish, a male of the first year: ye shall take it out from the sheep, or from the goats: :6 And ye shall **keep it up until the fourteenth day** of the same month: and the whole assembly of the congregation of Israel **shall kill it in the evening**. 7 And they **shall take of the blood, and strike it on the two side posts and on the upper door post of the houses,** wherein they shall eat it. 8 And they shall eat the flesh **in that night**, roast with fire, and unleavened bread; and with bitter herbs they shall eat it*

*Exo 12:13 And **the blood shall be to you for a token** upon the houses where ye are: and when I see the blood, I* *will pass over you, and the plague shall not be upon you to destroy you, when I smite the land of Egypt. 14 And **this day shall be unto you for a memorial**; and ye shall keep it a feast to YHVH throughout your generations; ye shall keep it a feast by an ordinance for ever.*

The next day – the 15th – was the first day of unleavened bread and the first day of freedom to leave that bondage.

*Exo 12:15 **Seven days shall ye eat unleavened bread**; even **the first day ye shall put away leaven out of your houses**: for whosoever eateth leavened bread **from the first day until the seventh day,** that soul shall be cut off from Israel. 16 And in the first day there shall be an holy convocation, and in the seventh day there shall be an holy convocation to you; no manner of work shall be done in them, save that which every man must eat, that only may be done of you. 17 And ye shall observe the feast of unleavened bread; **for in this selfsame day have I brought your armies out of the land of Egypt**: therefore shall ye observe this day in your generations by an ordinance forever.*

*Exo 12:22 And ye shall take a bunch of hyssop, and dip it in the blood that is in the bason, and strike the lintel and the two side posts with the blood that is in the bason; **and none of you shall go out at the door of his house until the morning.***

*Lev 23:5 In the **fourteenth day of the first month at even** is **YHVH's Passover**. 6 And on the **fifteenth day of the same month is the feast of unleavened bread** unto YHVH: seven days ye must eat unleavened bread. 7 In the first day* *ye shall have an holy convocation: ye shall do no servile work therein. 8 But ye shall offer an offering made by fire unto YHVH seven days: in the seventh day is an holy convocation: ye shall do no servile work therein.*

The day of First Fruits - the 16th -was introduced to the Israelites while on their journey through the wilderness.

*Lev 23:9 And YHVH spake unto Moses, saying, 10 Speak unto the children of Israel, and say unto them, When ye be come into the land which I give unto you, and shall reap the harvest thereof, **then ye shall bring a sheaf of the firstfruits** of your harvest unto the priest: 11 And he shall wave the sheaf before YHVH, to be accepted for you: **on the morrow after the sabbath the priest shall wave it.***

How do I know it was the next day? This was understood by the Jews. It was written in the Mishna, Philo, Josephus, and Talmud. Because He set these times down for us to observe, Yeshua HAD to fulfil them exactly. ***His blood shed on the cross was a token of our being purchased (redeemed) – 14th. He had no sin (leaven) as he was laid in the tomb – 15th. He was the Firstfruits from the dead – 16th.***

I also found and copied a few interesting quotes from some ante-Nicaean 'fathers' writings concerning the passion of our Master as follows:

FRAGMENTS OF CLEMENS ALEXANDRINUS.
Fragments Found in Greek Only in the Oxford Edition.

FROM THE LAST WORK ON THE PASSOVER. QUOTED IN THE PASCHAL CHRONICLE.

Accordingly, in the years gone by, Jesus went to eat the passover sacrificed by the Jews, keeping the feast. But when he had preached He who was the Passover, the Lamb of God, led as a sheep to the slaughter, presently **taught His disciples** the mystery of the type **on the thirteenth day,** on which also they inquired, "Where wilt Thou that we prepare for Thee to eat the passover?" **(Mat 26:17)** It was on this day, then, that both the consecration of the unleavened bread and the preparation for the feast took place. Whence John naturally describes the disciples as already previously prepared to have their feet washed by the Lord. **And on the following day our Saviour suffered,** He who was the Passover, propitiously sacrificed by the Jews.

THE SAME.

Suitably, therefore, **to the fourteenth day, on which He also suffered, in the morning,** the chief priests and the scribes, who brought Him to Pilate, did not enter the Praetorium, **that they might not be defiled, but might freely eat the passover in the evening.** With this precise determination of the days both the whole Scriptures agree, and the Gospels harmonize. The resurrection also attests it. **He certainly rose on the third day, which fell on the first day of the weeks of harvest, on which the law prescribed that the priest should offer up the sheaf.** (Which, according to Josephus was the 16th)

CONSTITUTIONS OF THE HOLY APOSTLES
7.07.09 XIV

153

CONCERNING THE PASSION OF OUR LORD, AND WHAT WAS DONE ON EACH DAY OF HIS SUFFERINGS

*For they began to hold a council against the Lord **on the second day of the week (the10th), in the first month,** which is Xanthicus; and the **deliberation continued on the third day of the week (the 11ᵗʰ); but on the fourth day (the 12ᵗʰ) they determined to take away His life by crucifixion....***

And on the fifth day of the week (the 13ᵗʰ), when we had eaten the Passover with Him, and when Judas had dipped his hand into the dish, and received the sop, and was gone out by night, the Lord said to us: "The hour is come that ye shall be dispersed, and shall leave me alone;"

*....in their madness cast upon Him, **till it was very early in the morning**, and then they lead Him away to Annas, who was father-in-law to Caiaphas; **and when they had done the like things to Him there, it being the day of the preparation (the 14ᵗʰ), they delivered Him to Pilate the Roman governor, ...***

*Pilate therefore, disgracing his authority by his pusillanimity, convicts himself of wickedness by regarding the multitude more than this just person, and bearing witness to Him that He was innocent, yet as guilty delivering Him up to the punishment of the cross, **although the Romans had made laws that no man unconvicted should be put to death....***

Then there was darkness for three hours, from the sixth to the ninth, and again light in the evening; as it is written: "It shall not be day nor night, and at the evening there shall be light." ....

*He gave up the ghost, **(Luk 23:46)** and was buried before sunset in a new sepulchre. **But when the first day of the week (the 16ᵗʰ) dawned He arose from the dead, and***

154

fulfilled those things which before His passion He foretold to us, saying: "The Son of man must continue in the heart of the earth three days and three nights." (Mat 12:40) And when He was risen from the dead, He appeared first to Mary Magdalene, and Mary the mother of James, then to Cleopas in the way, and after that to us His disciples, who had fled away for fear of the Jews, but privately were very inquisitive about Him. (Mar 16:9; Joh 20:11, etc.; Luk 24:18; Mar 16:14) But these things are also written in the Gospel.

IGNATIUS
VOL 1.04.04

On the day of the preparation, (the 14ᵗʰ) *then, at the third hour, He received the sentence from Pilate, the Father permitting that to happen; at the sixth hour* **He was crucified;** *at the ninth hour He gave up the ghost; He was taken down from the cross ,and laid in a new tomb.42* **During the Sabbath (the 15ᵗʰ)He continued under the earth** *in the tomb in which Joseph of Arimathaea had laid Him.* **At the dawning of the Lord's day (the 16ᵗʰ)He arose** *from the dead, according to what was spoken by Himself, "As Jonah was three days and three nights in the whale's belly, so shall the Son of man also be three days and three nights in the heart of the earth." (Mat_12:40)* **The day of the preparation, then, comprises the passion; the Sabbath embraces the burial; the Lord's Day contains the resurrection.**

Notice that two of these writers use the 3 days, 3 nights, but clearly show the whole event taking place from the 14th to the morning of the 16th. Obviously, they understood the true meaning of this quote.

I questioned why in the New Testament *this one Sabbath* was called great, but not the one starting Sukkot. I believe I found an answer in Leviticus 23. It was commanded to be observed as a memorial for their being set free from bondage – Just as Yeshua did descending into Sheol to preach to those imprisoned by sin and setting them free along with those still alive and then rising from the dead the next day which just happens to be Firstfruits!

*Co 15:20 But now is the Messiah risen from the dead, and become **the firstfruits of them that slept**. 21 For since by man came death, by man came also the resurrection of the dead. 22 For as in Adam all die, even so in the Messiah shall all be made alive. 23 But every man in his own order: **the Messiah the firstfruits**; afterward they that are the Messiahs at his coming.)*

He fulfilled all PERFECTLY and we can celebrate the memorial perfectly every year too according to YHWH's calendar. *Each year it never fails.*

There are those who argue that this 3 days 3 nights thing is why the lunar Sabbath calendar is no good. I would like to know **HOW** it works with the Roman (Gregorian) calendar. There is more confusion with it than with YHWH'S calendar according to the sun, moon and stars; in which there is NO confusion. *If the 14th is on Monday evening then you wait SIX days to start the omer count in order to follow the*

command to start counting the day after the Saturday Sabbath OR you ignore His instructions of "the day after" the Sabbath and begin the count on the 16th; as stated in Josephus, Philo, Mishna and Talmud. If He has all of His other commanded Feasts set to the days according to the counting of the moon month, why not His first Feast – The Sabbath?

For anyone to make the statement that it just **HAPPENED** to work out perfectly when Yeshua died is to say that YHWH doesn't care if we are put in confusion all the years before or after that event. If we are not to be able to understand the times, why then did Yeshua say:

Mat 16:1 And the Pharisees and Sadducees having come, tempting, did question him, to shew to them a sign from the heaven, 2 and he answering said to them, `Evening having come, ye say, Fair weather, for the heaven is red, 3 and at morning, Foul weather to-day, for the heaven is red--gloomy; **hypocrites, the face of the heavens indeed ye do know to discern, but the signs of the times ye are not able!**

Let's face it – It is always on the money with the calendar time piece set in motion on the 4th day of creation. Every Feast on its proper day at the proper time of the month.

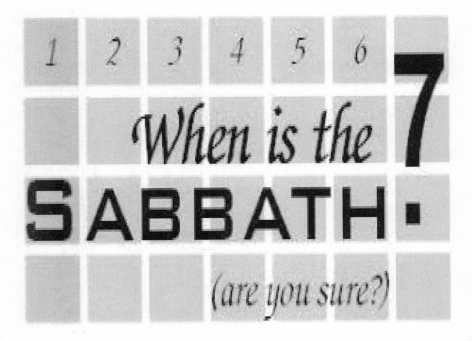

When is the SABBATH.
1 2 3 4 5 6 7
(are you sure?)

APPENDIX B

BUT, DIO CASSIUS SAID...

I hear this a lot when discussing YHWH's calendar. It is easy to get taken off to a side road and ambushed by the enemy of time – Ha Satan - if you do not understand your history.

Let's just take a stroll down the path of Dio Cassius's time and look for proper information to clarify what is going on.

Dio Cassius was a Roman statesman and historian of Greek origin born in 155 CE and died in 235 CE. His writing took place around 220 CE (3rd century). He was not even born at the time of Hadrian's expelling the Jews from Jerusalem, forbidding the reading of Torah and stopping their calendar. Dio never knew the Jews as a nation; nor was he aware of their ways according to their holy days. By 200 AD (3rd century) many Jews had abandoned many of the religious ways of their people and followed many Roman ways; even adjusting to the Roman calendar. What kind of calendar system did the Romans have at that time after the Bar Kokhba revolt (132–135 AD)?

The Julian calendar was the main Roman calendar at the time of Cassius, and the one he followed. The old Lunar Roman calendar with kalends, ides and nones reckoning was also still in use. There were a few other calendars in his territory being used too like the Macedonian, Egyptian, and Jewish (as beginning to fold into the Roman calendar). In 135 CE Hadrian forbid the use of the true Jewish calendar so through Cassius's life he was most likely not aware of that calendar.

The Julian calendar was at first side by side with the old lunar nundinal figuring, (which used the titles of Kalends (beginning of month), Nones (end of month), and Ides (middle of month) and there were still 8 days a week) and had letters for the 7 days. Remember the famous quote "beware the Ides of March" warning Julius Caesar who was assassinated in 44 BC. The nundinal cycle was eventually replaced by the seven-day week which **began with the day of Saturn.** This first came into use in Italy during the early imperial period in the 2nd century (100–199 CE). The system of nundinal letters was also adapted for the week.

FROM A CONTEMPORARY OF THE APOSTLE PAUL

*Petronius, the Roman satirist and voluptuary, who was once proconsul in Bithynia, and later consul there, was for some time an intimate associate of the Roman emperor Nero. (Later seeing himself fallen into disfavor and doomed to destruction by his imperial master, **he slit his veins and bled to death about 66 AD). Thus he died about the time that Nero had the apostle Paul beheaded.***

*One of the notable works composed by Petronius was a novel entitled The Banquet of Trimalchio, in which he pictures the luxury of the wealthy class of his time. This Trimalchio is represented as being a rich freedman who lived in southern Italy, probably at Puteoli or Cumae. In his description of the dining room, the writer said: "Two calendars were fixed on either doorpost, one having this entry, if I remember right: 'Our master C. is out to supper on December the 30th and 31st,' the other being painted with the Moon in her course, and the likenesses of the seven stars. Lucky and unlucky days were marked too with distinctive knobs." **This passage has been cited by many writers to show that the planetary week was in use in Roman calendars of the first century.** The description of the calendar, as given by Petronius, agrees in the minutest details with the facts as revealed by archaeology. The course of the Moon through the lunar month of thirty days was indicated from day to day by the knob (bulla) or stud fastened on a peg. By the side of each number of the days of the month there was a hole into which the peg could be inserted. **The seven days of the planetary week, from that of SATURN TO THAT OF VENUS, were represented by*** *likenesses (imagines) or images of these astrological deities. In stone calendars only their names appear, as a rule, but upon the household calendar tablets their images or pictures were painted. By the side of each planetary figure or name of the day there was a hole into which the peg with the knob could be inserted. This peg, which was often of brass, was moved from hole to hole each day, just as now we daily turn over a new leaf of our desk calendars in order to keep up to date with the weekly cycle.*

SUN-WORSHIP AND THE ORIGIN OF SUNDAY

Samuele Bacchiocchi, Ph. D., Andrews University

1. Two Sabine calendars found in central Italy in 1795 and a third one which came to light at Cimitele, near Nola in southern Italy, in 1956 (all three dated no later than the time of Tiberius (A.D. 14-37)(1ˢᵗ century), **present in the right column the eight letters from A to H of the eight-day Roman nundinum market week** *and in the left column the seven letters from A to G, representing the seven-day planetary week. In addition to these calendars should be considered also several so-called "indices nundinarii" (some of them dated in the early empire). These give the name of the towns* **and the corresponding days of the planetary week (WHICH ALWAYS STARTS WITH SATURDAY—dies Saturni) on which the market was to be held.**

2. Dio Cassius, Historia 49, 22, LCL 5, p. 389; cf. Historia 37, 16 and 37, 17; Josephus, Wars of the Jews 1, 7, 3 and Antiquities of the Jews 14, 4, confirms Dio Cassius's account, saying that the Romans succeeded in capturing the city **because they understood that Jews on the Sabbath only acted defensively.**

3. *According to the geocentric system of astronomy of that period, the order of the planets was as follows: Saturn (farthest), Jupiter, Mars, Sun, Venus, Mercury, and Moon (nearest).* **In the planetary week, however, the days are named after the planets in this sequence: SATURN,** *Sun, Moon, Mars, Mercury, Jupiter, and Venus; for a discussion, see R.L. Odom (fn. 35), pp. 11-17.*

4. *W. Rordorf, Sunday, p. 35;* **note that initially the day of the Sun was the second day of the planetary week, following the day of SATURN WHICH WAS FIRST.** *This is clearly proved, for instance, by several stone calendars (so-called indices nundinarii) where the days of the week are given horizontally,* **STARTING WITH THE DAY OF SATURN;** *see above fn. In a mural inscription found in Herculaneum the "Days of the Gods" are given in capital Greek letters,* **STARTING WITH "KRONOU [OF SATURN],** *Heliou [of Sun] . . ." (CIL IV, part 2, 582, no. 5202). A similar list was found in Pompeii written in Latin and* **BEGINNING WITH "SATURNI [OF SATURN]"** *(CIL IV, part 2, 712, no. 6779). W. Rordorf, Sunday, p. 35, rightly stresses this point:* **"It must, however, be emphasized straight away that in the planetary week Sunday always occupied only the second place in the sequence of days."**

5. *The existence and common use of the planetary week already in the first century A.D. are well attested by several testimonies. In the present study we need refer only to a few of them. The Roman* **historian Dio Cassius, who wrote his Roman History between A.D. 200-220, reports that**

Jerusalem was captured both by Pompey in 63 B.C. and by Gaius Sosius in 37 B.C. "on the day even then called the day of Saturn." That the praxis of naming the days of the week after the planetary deities was already in use before Christ is further corroborated by the contemporary references of Horace (ca. 35 B.C.) to "dies Jovis— Thursday" and of Tibullus (ca. B.C. 29-30) to dies Saturni—Saturday."

6. *Petronius, a Roman satirist (died ca. **A.D. 66**) in his novel The Banquet of Trimalchio describes a stick calendar which Trimalchio had affixed on the doorpost with the number of the days on the side and "the likeness of the seven stars" on the other side. A knob was inserted in the respective holes to indicate the date and the day. **Sextus Julius Frontinus_(ca. A.D. 35-103**), a Roman soldier and writer, in his work The Stratagems, referring to the fall of Jerusalem of A.D. 70, writes that Vespasian "attacked the Jews on the day of Saturn, on which it is forbidden for them to do anything serious and defeated them."*

Let's try to put some pieces together here regarding dates in time. I have numbered the paragraphs from the chapter "Sun Worship and the Origin of Sunday" to make it easier to reference.

In paragraphs **1, 3 and 4.** We can see that into the 1st century AD the eight day week of Rome was still in use WITH Saturn day as the first day of the week. If we skip down to paragraph **5.** We will see that the historical events Cassius is reporting on are in **BC which put Saturn day on the first day of the week,** since it was in that position still in the 1st century AD.

In paragraph **6.** You still have the stick calendar being used in 66 AD which puts it in the time of Frontinus.

So what is he really saying in his statement about the attack from Vespasian? Obviously he too did not understand that only the preparation for battle (ramparts built, etc.) took place on the Jews Sabbath (for they would fight defensively on that day if attacked) and it was the next day they were attacked and defeated – which was the day of Saturn. (This we will read about by Josephus farther on.) That was only 4 years after the death of Petronius who was still very familiar with the stick calendar.

Below: picture of Roman stick calendar. First figure (day one) is the picture of Saturn with sickle in hand.

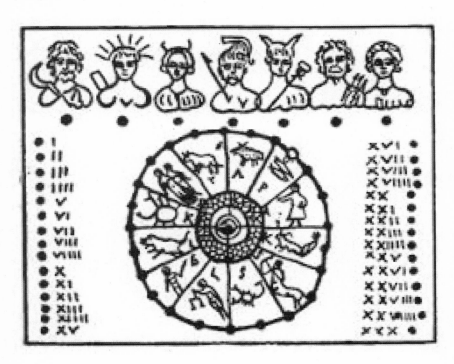

Now look at a section out of "Rest Days" by Webster Hutton:

REST DAYS

The planetary week, an institution which has spread eastward over the Oriental world and westward into Europe, is a product of the speculations of astrologers and philosophers during the Hellenistic, or Greco-Oriental, era. **The sequence of its days depends ultimately upon the order of the seven planetary spheres, adopted by Ptolemy (100 – 170 ce)** in antiquity and after him by astronomers until the discoveries of Copernicus. If the planets are grouped according to their distance from the earth, beginning with the highest and descending to the lowest, we obtain the following order: Saturn, Jupiter, Mars, Sun, Venus, Mercury, Moon. No certain evidence exists that this arrangement was known at an earlier date than the second century before our era.^ The astrological order, **WHICH ALSO BEGINS WITH SATURN**, proceeds next to the fourth planet, or Sun, from which again the fourth planet (by inclusive reckoning) is the Moon. By continuing to select every fourth planet thereafter we obtain at length the regents **of the seven weekdays : Saturn, Sun, Moon, Mars, Mercury, Jupiter, Venus.** How, it may be asked, did such an arrangement arise? **This question has been answered for us by the Roman historian, Dio Cassius,** who interrupts his narrative of the victorious campaign of Pompey the Great in Palestine to furnish a brief account of the planetary week.^ The institution, says Dio Cassius, can be explained In two ways. According to the first explanation the gods are supposed to preside over separate days of the week, following the ^"principle of the tetrachord' (which is believed to constitute the basis of music)." The second *explanation given by Dio Cassius, and also by Vettius Valens, is connected with the astrological theory of "chronocratorles," which assigned to the several planets dominion over hours and days as periods of time.*

The diagram illustrates **Dio Cassius's first explanation of the astrological week in use among the Romans,** *the assignment of the days to the planetary gods according to the musical harmony "by fours" (or the tetra-chord). The celestial order of the planets follows the circle:* **Saturn, Jupiter, Mars, Sun, Venus, Mercury, and Moon**. *The daily order follows the arrow in the star pattern, and the musical theory works thus by intervals of fours:* **(1) Saturn, Jupiter, Mars, (2) Sun, Venus, Mercury, (3) Moon, Saturn, Jupiter, (4) Mars, Sun, Venus, (5) Mercury, Moon, Saturn, (6) Jupiter, Mars, Sun, (7) Venus, Mercury, Moon, etc.**

This diagram shows the planetary gods of the days of the week in accordance with Dio Cassius's first explanation. The planetary deities are listed in their supposedly celestial order. Taking them according to the musical theory of the tetra-chord, every fourth god is given his day.

Listed below are more proofs of Saturn being the first day of the Roman pagan week started at the time of the Caesars.

THE PLANETARY WEEK IN THE FIRST CENTURY BC

THERE has not yet appeared any evidence to indicate that the pagan week of days named after the seven planetary deities was in use among the Romans during the period of the Republic. 'The testimony of both the classical *writers and the archaeological discoveries **points to the first century before Christ as the time when it was adopted by the Roman people**. Not a few 1 are the scholars who think that it came to Rome about the time when Julius Caesar was Pontifex Maximus (63-44 BC)*

CLEMENT OF ALEXANDRIA

*Josephus, a contemporary of the apostle john, had a similar notion about the candlestick of the temple and the seven planets. Ptolemy (in the first half of the second century AD) held that the **order of the planets was thus: Saturn, Jupiter, Mars, Sun, Venus, Mercury, Moon.** This was the Babylonian arrangement. Clement of Alexandria (about 200 AD) Evidently did the same, for he placed the Sun in the central position. Speaking of the candlestick in the temple, he said that "by it were shown the motions of the seven planets, that perform their revolutions towards the south. For three branches rose on either side of the lamp, and lights on them; since also the Sun, like the lamp, set in the midst of all the planets, dispenses with a kind of divine music the light to those above and to those below." Thus the Babylonian astronomical science of the planetary bodies prevailed among the Greeks and Romans at the beginning of the Christian Era.*

A GOLDEN BRACELET

*Another item is a golden bracelet found in Syria, and said to be preserved in the British Museum. In this case we have the names of the planetary gods in Greek, together with their likenesses, **in the exact order as they occur in the pagan week**. Victor Durtly describes it:*

"This little bracelet is only two and a third inches in diameter, and the engraved figures are but two fifth's of an inch. **The careless workmanship marks the period as near the close of the third or the beginning of the fourth century (250-300 AD).** On the eight faces of the octagon are engraved the seven gods or goddesses of the week, and **Fortune, TYXH [TUCHE], which opens the series. She holds in the right hand a cornucopia, and rests the left hand upon a rudder. Saturn, KPONOY. [KRONOS], comes next in order.** He is clad in a long garment, and with the left hand holds a scarf which is floating above his head. The third place is occupied by the Sun, HALOY. [HELIOS], radiate, and standing in a chariot with two horses. He holds in the right hand a whip, and in the left a globe. The Moon, ZAHNH [SELENE], is the fourth figure. She wears a double tunic, a double crescent is on her head, and a veil, puffed out by the wind; she holds a lighted torch in her right hand. After the Moon comes Mars, APHI [ARES], naked helmeted, carrying his buckler. The sixth figure is Mercury

THE PLANETARY GODS IN A BOAT

A small bronze boat of the Roman period was discovered in Montpelier, France, and it is shown **carrying the busts of the seven gods of the planetary week in their correct order.** Bernard de Montfaucon, already mentioned, gives the following description of this object:

"An antique brass monument in M. Bon's cabinet, is the only curiosity I have yet seen, where the week is represented in emblem. **The gods, which preside over the seven days of the week, and from whom they derived their names, are there arranged in order, as in a boat. There SATURN HAS THE FIRST PLACE,** agreeable to what

168

Macrobius says in Scipio's dream, that Saturn's is the first of the seven spheres.... His visage looks old, and he is, as Cicero observes, sated with years. Next to him is Sol or the Sun, which passed in later ages for Apollo.

"Joseph Fuchs, Gesch. von Mainz 2, 27 seq. (Kupfert 4, Number 7)," says Jacob Grimm, "describes a Roman round altar, **probably of the third or fourth century, on which are carved the seven gods of the week (1 Saturn, 2 Apollo, 3 Diana, 4 Mars, 5 Mercury, 6 Jupiter, 7 Venus),** and in the eighth place a genius." This altar was found in Swabia, Germany.

A STICK CALENDAR

At Pausilypuni, near Puteoli (in Italy), there was found in 1891 a tomb which was partly covered by a large flat stone of marble that once was part of a nundinal calendar on which the days of the week, after the pagan style, played a part. **The top line of the fragment gives the Latin of the planetary names of the days in their genitive forms: "Saturni, Solis, Lunae, Martis."** The names Mercury, Jupiter, and Venus were broken off. Below the line of the names of the days of the week appear the names of Roman cities where the markets were held in turn, three of which are broken off. Above the name of each day of the week there is a hole drilled into the marble slab, for the insertion of a brass peg for marking the days. Also a hole appears above each city where the market was held, for distinguishing them by the use of a peg. The archaeologists report that in these holes they have discovered stains of oxidized brass, and that these vestiges indicate that pegs of this material were used for insertion in the holes. Therefore this type of register is known as a "stick calendar."

ANOTHER STICK CALENDAR

Another interesting fragment of a Roman stick calendar which served to indicate the days of the week after the pagan mode, is that found a long time ago by Fulvius Ursinus, and is now said to be preserved in the Museum of Naples (Italy). The very name of Rome is listed among the cities where the markets were held. At the top may be seen the names of the last three days of the pagan week, **which were inscribed thus: (SATURN, SOLAR, LUNAR, MARS, MERCURY, JOVIS, VENUS).** The first four and part of the fifth are broken off

AN ENGRAVED STONE

Victor Duruy, the French historian, has described an engraved stone **of the Roman period**, which shows the seven planetary gods in the exact order as they appear in the pagan week. Each of them is designated by the initial letter of his name in Latin. Duruy speaks of it as an "engraved stone in the collection of Mr. Maxwell Sommerville. **The gods which preside over the days of the week, walking to the right, have over their heads inscribed the initial letters of each one's name (Saturn, Helios,** Luna or Diana, Mars, Mercury, Jupiter, Venus). Saturn is veiled like a priest, the Sun has the radiate crown, Diana has the curved veil above her head, Mars is armed and helmeted, Mercury wears the winged cap, Jupiter holds the scepter, and Venus the apple."

POMPEY IN 63 BC

After Queen Salonic Alexandra, ruler of the Jews, died in **70 BC**, there arose a dispute about which of her two sons should succeed her. The Pharisees supported the cause of Aristobulus 11, while the Sadducees were on the side of Hyrcanus 11. Aristobulus appealed by letter to Pompey, the great Roman consul, to arbitrate in the matter. Pompey was at that time occupied in a military campaign in Asia, but when he came to Damascus he received the envoys of the rival brothers. However, he delayed in making a decision, and Aristobulus, becoming impatient, assumed the power at Jerusalem. This act of disrespect angered the Roman general and brought him to a decision at once. He proceeded immediately to the Jewish capital and besieged the city for three months.

Dio Cassius, a Roman historian who wrote in Greek (about 230 AD), explains the strategy employed by Pompey in taking Jerusalem. He says:

"If they [the Jews] had continued defending it [the temple] on all days alike, he could not have got possession of it. As it was, they made an exception of what are called the days of Saturn, and by doing no work at all on those days afforded the Romans an opportunity in this interval to batter down the wall. The latter, on learning of this superstitious awe of theirs, made no serious attempts the rest of the time, but on those days, when they came around in succession, assaulted most vigorously. Thus the defenders were captured on the day of Saturn without making any defense, and all the wealth was plundered. The kingdom was given to Hyrcanus, and Aristobulus was carried away."

DIO CASSIUS'S TESTIMONY CONFIRMED

The important fact for us to note in this story of the capture of Jerusalem by Pompey in 63 BC **is that the day of Saturn in the planetary week of the pagans then corresponded to the Sabbath or seventh day of the Biblical week of the Jews**. The testimony of Dio Cassius is confirmed by that of Josephus, the Hebrew historian, who was a contemporary of the apostles. **Josephus's account of the siege runs thus:**

"Nor had the Romans succeeded in their endeavors, **had not Pompey taken notice** of the seventh days, on which the Jews abstain from all sorts of work on a religious account, and raised his bank, **but restrained his soldiers from fighting on those days**; for the Jews only acted defensively on Sabbath days."

"Had it not been for our practice, from the days of our forefathers, to rest on the seventh day, this bank [thrown up by Pompey] could never have been perfected, by reason of the opposition the Jews would have made; **for though our law gives us leave then to defend ourselves against those that begin to fight us and assault us, yet does it not permit us to meddle with our enemies while they do anything else.** Which thing when the Romans understood, on those days which we call Sabbaths they threw nothing at the Jews, nor came to any pitched battle with them; but raised up their earthen banks, and brought their engines into such forwardness, **that they might do execution the next day**. The city was taken on the third month, **on the day of the fast,** upon the hundred and seventy-ninth olympiad, when Caius Antonius and Marcus Tullius Cicero were consuls."

(the Jews did not fast on the weekly Sabbath it was the next day.)

Josephus adds, in the same account, that his testimony was confirmed by the writings of Strabo, Nicolaus of Damascus, and Titus Livius (Livy).

Strabo, the Greek geographer who was born perhaps in the year that Pompey captured Jerusalem, wrote thus: "Pompey seized the city, it is said, after watching for the day of fasting, when the Judaeans were abstaining from all work; he filled up the trench and threw ladders across it."

Okay, let us examine the information of the fall of Jerusalem from both Dio Cassius and Josephus.

First of all look at how Josephus phrases things. He does not use the names of the pagan days. He only says *"had not Pompey **taken notice** of the seventh days, on which the Jews abstain from all sorts of work on a religious account."* Now why would he say that **IF** the Jews were using Saturday as their Sabbath day every week? Also, Pompey would already know which day it was if it was always on Saturday. He wouldn't have to "take notice"

Also, he says that, *"**on those days which we call Sabbaths they threw nothing at the Jews, nor came to any pitched battle with them**; but raised up their earthen banks, and brought their engines into such forwardness, **that they might do execution the next day**"*

Now if you reread what Dio says, you notice his claim of the battle taking place on the Jews Sabbath which he proclaimed to be the day of Saturn… which was really the day AFTER the Jews Sabbath that they were taken. Going back to the 4th page in this writing, you will read the explanation of Dio of the order of the days by their pagan names; *which just happens to be starting with Saturn!* I also have a big question here. Why is the word of a man, who not only hated the Jews, and was writing his historical events at a time way after Hadrian in 135 AD forbid the use of the Hebrew calendar and banned all Jews from even seeing Jerusalem, but also never saw Jerusalem himself, being taken as absolute correctness; when it obviously does not coincide with the account of Josephus who was as a matter of fact a Jew?

Both times in history that Jerusalem was taken, it was said to be at times when the pagan week began with Saturn. However, in 63 BC the Julian calendar was not in existence with the names of the days of the week. Only the old nundinal calendar existed with 10 months and 8 letters for the days. The Julian was created by Julius Caesar in 45 BC with still only letters for the days and 10 months. The two more months of September and October were added by Caesar Augustus. It would be very tricky indeed for Dio to go back in time to get the day the 63 BC battle took place with much accuracy.

Let us read a few more tidbits concerning the calendar of Rome:

In 1795 were found the marble fragments of what is known as the **Sabine Calendar (Fasti Sabini),** in a place in central Italy. These portions represent the months of September and October in the Julian calendar. The experts in this type of archaeological finds have declared them to **belong to the reign of Augustus Caesar, and that they were in use between 19 BC and 4 AD** (that is, between the years 735 and 757 of the foundation of the city of Rome). The first column, of figures, indicates the days of the month in their numerical order. The second column, of capital letters, shows the seven days of the week in their order, as follows: A, B, C, D, E, F, G. The third column lists in order, by the letters A, B, C, D, E, F, G, and H the recurrence of the market days, which were called nundinae. These are thus called because according to common Roman reckoning the market day came around every ninth (nonus) day, but according to our common mode of complication they fell every eight days.

The following statement by Herbert Thurston, a well known Roman Catholic authority, makes a very enlightening reference to this Sabine Calendar: **"When the Oriental seven day period, or week, was introduced, in the time of Augustus, the first seven letters of the alphabet were employed in the same way [as done for the nundinae],** to indicate the days of this new division of time. In fact, fragmentary calendars on marble still survive in which both a cycle of eight letters-A to H-indicating mindinae, and a cycle of seven letters-A to G -indicating weeks, are used side by side (see 'Corpus Inscriptionum Latinarum,' 2d ed., 1, 220. The same peculiarity occurs in the Philocalian Calendar of **AD 356 [354],** ibid., p. 256). This device was imitated by the Christians, and in their calendars the days of the year from 1 January to 31

December were marked with a continuous recurring cycle of seven letters: A, B, C, D, E, F, G"

Remember that in 325 AD Constantine changed the Roman calendar to what we see now. Sunday was placed as the first day of the week and Saturday became the last and Dio Cassius was already dead.

*Marcion and some others in the **second century had observed the Sabbath by fasting on it out of contempt for the Jews and their God.** The Gnostics had affirmed that the Father of Jesus Christ was not the Jehovah of the Old Testament. Now Sylvester and his associates attempted to make Sunday, which hitherto had been a merry ecclesiastical festival, a day of solemn rest superior to the Sabbath. Hence, **not only Sunday was decreed to be a day of general rest throughout the Roman Empire, by the laws of Constantine, but also the Sabbath was decreed to be a day of fasting by the bishop of Rome***

A POMPEIIAN PAINTING OF THE PLANETARY GODS

Furthermore, there have been preserved for it's at least two sets of Roman pictures depicting the seven planetary gods of the days of the pagan week in their calendar order. They were painted before the eruption of Vesuvius in 79 AD.

One set of these, in the form of medallions, was found by excavators in Pompeii in 1760, on the wall of a room and by good fortune completely intact. This set is preserved in the museum at Naples. In their original setting, the gods of the days of the pagan week appear in the following order: SATURN, Sun, Moon, Mars, Mercury, Jupiter, and Venus.

TREASURES FROM POMPEII AND HERCULANEUM

On August 24, 79 AD, just nine years after the fall of Jerusalem, Mount Vesuvius, located about seven miles southeast of Naples, Italy, suddenly erupted and buried three towns tinder a heavy rain of lava and ashes. These towns were Pompeii, Herculaneum, and Stabiae. In this calamity perished Drusilla, the wife of Felix, the governor who trembled as he heard the apostle Paul reason at the bar of the court in Caesarea. The son of Felix and Drusilla lost his life also in this catastrophe.

The burial of those ancient towns under a blanket of volcanic ash has been the means of preserving for our day much information about the Roman ways of living in the first century, knowledge which otherwise might have perished under the ravages of time and man's barbarities. Pompeii and Herculaneum have been among the most fruitful sources of data about the planetary week in Roman times.

"DAYS OF THE GODS"

In Herculaneum, for example, there was found inscribed in Greek upon a wall a list which was entitled "Days of the Gods, in capital letters. Underneath this title there appears in the same language, and in capital letters also, the names of the seven planetary deities in the genitive form and **in the exact order of the days** in the astrological week, as follows:

KRONOU (OF SATURN), *Heliou (of Sun), Selenes (of Moon), Areos (of Mars), Hermou (of Mercury), Dios (of Jupiter), and Aphrodeites (of Venus). The letter r of Hermes, and the letters Aphro of Aphrodite, were damaged so as to be illegible, but all the rest of the inscription was so plainly visible as to leave no room for doubt about the spelling of the words.*

Another inscription, found in Pompeii and written in Latin, contains a list of the planetary gods in the order of the days of the pagan week, as follows: Saturni (of Saturn), Solis (of the Sun), Lunae (of the Moon), Martis (of Mars), the name of Mercury is missing, Jovis (of Jupiter), and Veneris (of Venus). These names were inscribed in capital letters, but no title is given to the list as in the preceding case.

So then, having all this evidence of the first day of the week being Saturn until the time of Constantine, do you still want to quote Dio Cassius?

MY CONCLUSION

After reading this book, many of you would probably ask "what difference does it make?" "Does it really matter that we follow the lunar based Sabbath?" "Who honestly cares?" "It only causes division among YHWH's believers, and we should be striving for unity instead."

My response to these thoughts is; if you don't think it matters that you get the right day for His Sabbath, then why did you leave Sunday (causing strife with family) and go to Saturday? Why are you so adamant about Sabbath being every seventh day of the week? Most Christians go Sunday and wait seven days till the next Sunday. Muslims go Friday and wait seven more days till the next Friday. All three of these "seven day sabbaths" (Friday, Saturday, Sunday) are based on the pagan Roman calendar. And why then, did you walk away from Christmas and Easter after realizing they weren't His Feast days, and risked division with loved ones to obey YHWH? I would urge you to think carefully before standing on the conclusion that it causes too much disunity and therefore would displease Father. If it truly is His Sabbath that He set up at the beginning, then following His calendar would not displease Him. Yeshua said "Do not think that I came to bring peace on the earth; I did not come to bring peace, but a sword. "For I came to SET A MAN AGAINST HIS FATHER, AND A DAUGHTER AGAINST HER MOTHER, AND A DAUGHTER-IN-LAW AGAINST HER MOTHER-IN-LAW; and A MAN'S ENEMIES WILL BE THE MEMBERS OF HIS HOUSEHOLD. He who loves father or mother more than Me is not worthy of Me; and he who loves son or daughter more than Me is not worthy of Me. Matthew 10:34-37

When we follow the truth, there will be a battle. We just must stay gentle in spirit with those who react violently with our decision and be patient while YHWH works with them too.

Keeping Sabbath according to His time piece – sun, moon and stars – will truly set us apart from the world and make us stand out as His people.

Exo 20:8 "Remember the Sabbath day, to set it apart."

May YHWH be with you always and give you peace as you follow His ways.

Shalom, Diane